Despite the 'best before' dates on packets of rice stretching for months or years, in Asia the freshest rice is considered the best, and 'new season' or 'new crop' rice is highly prized. It's thought that the aromas dissipate over time, which affects the flavour of the rice. On the other hand, exceptional crops of basmati rice are aged to intensify the flavour and are sold as 'vintages', with an accompanying price tag.

The absorption method is considered the best way of cooking rice. You simply pour over boiling water so that the water level comes about 1cm/½in above the rice, bring to the boil, pop on a lid and turn the heat down to its lowest setting, then cook until the water has been absorbed and the rice is almost cooked. Turn off the heat and leave the rice to finish cooking in the steam, making sure you keep the lid on the pan. Cooking rice in this way gives you fluffy, separate grains.

Unfortunately, there isn't a general rule for the ratio of water to rice or cooking times, but usually you'll need about one and a half times water to rice. For wholegrain you'll probably need more as it takes longer to cook, and for short grain slightly less. If in doubt use less water at the start as you can always add more – you don't want to end up with stodgy mush. And add salt to the pot, as seasoning the rice brings out the flavour.

If you pre-soak your rice it will need less cooking time and less water. Soaking overnight is best (if you have time), but even just a 15-minute soak will make the grains more digestible.

There are a few food safety considerations to take note of. If cooked rice is left at room temperature for an extended period, the rice can harbour bacteria, which if consumed can make you ill. To avoid this, if you're not eating cooked rice straight away, cool it as quickly as possible: spreading it out on a tray in a thin layer is a good way of doing this, or running it under cold water. As soon as it has reached room temperature, cover and refrigerate. You can store it for up to two days and either eat it cold or reheat it. Alternatively, you can freeze cooked rice; make sure you defrost it thoroughly in the fridge, then reheat until piping hot all the way through before eating. And don't forget, never reheat rice more than once.

TYPES OF RICE
★
FOR COOKING

Pudding rice
This isn't really a specific type of rice, but is white short-grain rice sold under the name 'pudding rice'. The term is rarely used outside the UK. When cooked with milk or water the rice becomes sticky and creamy. The grains are very absorbent and so a small amount of rice in proportion to liquid is used during cooking.

Thai sticky or glutinous rice
A medium-to-long-grain rice hailing from South East and East Asia. Glutinous rice does not actually contain gluten, but the name refers to the rice's glue-like sticky quality, which easily binds it into rice balls and cakes. It's best soaked in cold water for at least three hours, or overnight if you can, before cooking – steaming is the preferred method.

Thai black sticky or glutinous rice
Black sticky rice is a wholegrain rice (meaning the bran has not been removed), is purplish-black in colour and has a chewy texture. Pick up a bag in Asian supermarkets or order online. Like other unmilled rices, it takes longer to cook than white varieties.

Arborio rice
The most well-known of risotto rices (also used for making rice puddings), this plump, medium-grain rice from the Northern Italian region of Piedmont has a high starch content, which means it's wonderfully creamy when cooked. For a risotto it has to be cooked al dente, or with the centre of the grains still firm to the bite, otherwise you're just not doing it justice. If overcooked it becomes stodgy and porridge-like.

Carnaroli rice
A medium-grain Italian rice also used for making risotto and rice puddings. It has a higher starch content and firmer texture than Arborio rice, it is therefore a little more forgiving and keeps its shape better when cooked.

Basmati rice (white)
This fragrant, slender long-grain rice is grown in the Himalayan foothills and is considered to be one of the best-quality white rices. It has a distinctive aroma reminiscent of the pandan leaf, and the grains are separate, light and fluffy once cooked. It's most widely used in Indian, Pakistani and Middle-Eastern cuisines.

Basmati rice (wholegrain)

Nuttier and firmer in texture than white basmati and higher in nutrients, the outermost layer (the husk) of the rice has been removed but the grains still have all their layers of bran intact. To get white basmati rice, these layers of bran need to be removed by milling.

Paella rice

Again, this isn't actually a rice variety but the name used for types of rice suitable for cooking paella. Spanish bomba or Calasparra rice are the kings of paella rice and amongst the most expensive in Spain. The medium grains are pearl white in colour and have the ability to absorb lots of liquid, so really take on the flavour of the cooking stock.

American long-grain rice

An extremely versatile rice that's popular throughout the world. The grain is four to five times longer than it is wide. Most varieties are grown in America, and it's available as regular long-grain or easy-cook (or converted) rice.

Long-grain wholegrain rice

This rice has a really nutty flavour and slightly chewy texture. Only the husk is removed during milling so the bran layer remains, making this rice higher in fibre, vitamins and minerals. Because of this, it takes longer to soften and cook than white rice.

Jasmine rice (white)

Jasmine rice is a long-grain rice, also known as Thai fragrant rice. It doesn't actually have a jasmine flavour or scent, but it does have a subtle floral aroma when cooked. The aromas dissipate over time, so the new harvest crop is highly sought after. The grains are slightly sticky, so if using for fried rice, it should be cooked, cooled and chilled overnight first.

Jasmine rice (wholegrain)

Still with its bran layer, brown jasmine rice has a delicate floral aroma, slightly oaty taste and firm texture. Like other wholegrain rices, it's higher in fibre and nutrients than white jasmine rice. Use whenever you'd normally use the white variety, but make sure you cook it for a little longer.

Wild rice

Wild rice is actually the seed of a strain of aquatic grass grown mainly in North America. The grains are long, thin and black or brown in colour. It's a very good source of protein and is high in antioxidants. The grains are nutty and smoky, and have a chewy outer layer and tender inside. They pop open and 'flower' when cooked.

Japanese or sushi rice

Short-grain Japanese rice is a staple of the Japanese diet. There are many varieties, including Koshihikari, Hitomebore and Akitakomachi, but in supermarkets you'll often find it labelled as sushi rice. When cooked, it becomes sticky and can be easily rolled into balls or shaped into sushi, but it's also great served as a side.

Short-grain rice (white)

This rice is so plump it's almost round. The grains have a high starch content, which means they become sticky once cooked. It can be used for many dishes, including rice pudding, sushi and risotto. It's a very thirsty rice.

Short-grain rice (wholegrain)

Rich, chewy and nutty, wholegrain short-grain rice takes longer to cook and is less sticky than its white counterpart, but the grains still cling together. It's higher in nutrients, too.

Camargue red rice

This rice is grown in the marshes of the Camargue in South West France – there's even a rice museum there dedicated to the stuff. The outer bran layer of these wholegrains is red, which gives the rice its colour. It has a nutty taste and slightly chewy texture.

Black rice

There are various varieties and names for this medium-grain rice, including forbidden rice, Thai black rice, Nerone black rice and Venere black rice. All are high in fibre and have a mild, nutty taste. The grains are very high in antioxidants, containing as much or more than the levels found in blueberries. The new superfood?

Puffed brown rice

This is simply puffed wholegrain brown rice. It's light, crispy and good for you. Just don't get it confused with the white puffed rice packed with sugar, sweeteners and other unknowns.

A note on easy-cook (converted) rice

Many varieties of rice are available as easy-cook rice, but this doesn't mean the rice takes less time to cook. The name refers to the par-cooking of the rice after harvesting, prior to removing the husk. The effect is that the grains absorb many of the nutrients from the husk and the rice doesn't stick together or go soggy when you cook it at home.

RICE

★

VARIETIES

Wholegrain basmati rice

Short-grain brown rice

Pudding rice

Short-grain white rice

Japanese sushi rice

Thai black sticky or
glutinous rice

Thai sticky or
glutinous rice

Puffed brown rice

Camargue red rice

Wholegrain jasmine rice

White basmati rice

Paella rice

Wild rice

White jasmine rice

American long-grain rice

Long-grain wholegrain

Carnaroli rice

Arborio rice

Black rice

SALADS &

★

BOWLS

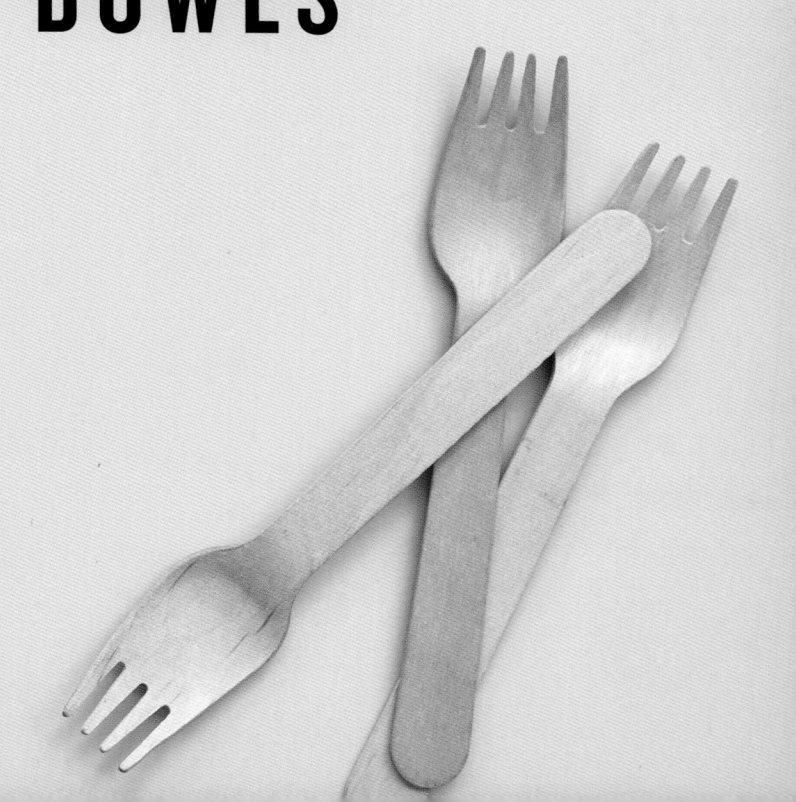

AVOCADO, SALMON &
SESAME RICE BOWL

Try shaping your avocado slices into a rose, or if life's too short, serve in slices on top of the rice.

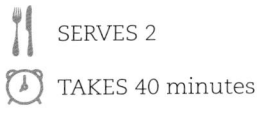 SERVES 2

TAKES 40 minutes

150g/1 cup short-grain brown rice
1 tbsp toasted sesame seeds
100g/4oz edamame beans, defrosted if frozen
1 avocado
1 fillet (about 90g/3oz) hot smoked salmon
handful coriander (cilantro) leaves, roughly chopped
salt

For the dressing
1 tbsp sesame oil
1 tbsp soy sauce
1 tbsp mirin
½ heaped tsp grated ginger
drizzle of honey

Cook the rice in salted water according to the packet instructions. Drain, then spread it out on a tray and leave to cool. Meanwhile, mix together the dressing ingredients in a small bowl.

Tip the rice into a bowl, then stir through the dressing, most of the sesame seeds and the edamame beans. Divide between bowls.

Halve the avocado, remove the stone and peel off the skin. Place an avocado half cut-side down on a chopping board, then slice very thinly across its width. With the slices remaining standing as they are, gently fan them to form a line of slices. Starting at one end, carefully roll up the line to form a rose shape and place it on top of the rice.

Flake over the salmon, then scatter the coriander and remaining sesame seeds on top.

CURRIED

★

RICE

A retro salad that makes a great BBQ side. The green pepper adds crunch, the dried fruit sweetness, and it's all brought together with a curry-powder-spiked dressing.

SERVES 4

TAKES 30 minutes

200g/1 cup plus 2 tbsp
   basmati rice
1 green (bell) pepper, deseeded
   and finely chopped
1 small red onion, finely chopped
½ bunch parsley, finely chopped
50g/2oz dried apricots, sliced
50g/2oz raisins
½ bunch parsley
25g/1oz flaked almonds, toasted
salt and freshly ground
   black pepper
For the dressing
4 tbsp extra virgin olive oil
1 tbsp white wine vinegar
1 garlic clove, crushed
1 tbsp lemon juice
¼ tsp sugar
1 tsp curry powder

Cook the rice in salted water according to the packet instructions. Drain, then spread it out on a tray and leave to cool. Meanwhile, mix together the dressing ingredients in a small bowl and season well.

Transfer the rice to a large bowl. Add the green pepper, onion, most of the parsley, the apricots and raisins. Finely chop most of the parsley and add this to the bowl, pour over the dressing and mix everything together. Tear over the remaining parsley and scatter with the flaked almonds before serving.

CHIPOTLE

★

BURRITO BOWLS

Burritos are delicious, but they're even better without the wrap as you get more of the filling! These bowls are gluten-free, too.

🍴 SERVES 2

⏰ TAKES 50 minutes

1 large chicken breast
2 tbsp chipotle paste
2 tbsp olive oil
zest and juice 1 lime
75g/⅓ cup long-grain rice
200g/7oz can black beans,
    rinsed and drained
1 garlic clove, crushed
125g/4½oz tomatoes,
    roughly chopped
½ red onion, finely chopped
small bunch coriander
    (cilantro) leaves
1 avocado, roughly chopped
handful little gem leaves,
    shredded
3 tbsp soured cream
25g/1oz mature Cheddar,
    grated (optional)
salt and freshly ground
    black pepper

Place the chicken breast between pieces of clingfilm and, using a rolling pin, bash to 1cm/½in thick. Mix the chipotle paste, 1 tsp of the oil, the zest and juice ½ lime and some salt together in a bowl, then add the chicken and stir to coat. Chill for 30 minutes. Cook the rice in salted water according to the packet instructions.

Heat 1 tbsp of the oil in a non-stick frying pan over a high heat, add the black beans and fry for 3 minutes until beginning to crisp. Stir through the garlic, then tip in the rice and season well. Divide between serving bowls.

Combine the tomatoes, onion, coriander and a pinch of salt in a bowl. In a separate bowl, mix together the avocado, zest and juice ½ lime and some seasoning.

Heat the remaining oil in the frying pan. Add the chicken and fry for 2½–3 minutes on each side until cooked through. Set aside to rest, then slice. Spoon the tomato salsa, avocado and lettuce into the bowls with the rice. Top with the chicken, dollop over a spoonful of soured cream and sprinkle with the Cheddar.

RED RICE

★

RADISH & PEA SALAD

Ricotta salata is an aged, hard version of ricotta, which is drier and saltier than its fresh cousin. It goes well with the sweetness of the peas and the oily dressing.

🍴 SERVES 4

⏰ TAKES 50 minutes

200g/1 cup, plus 1 tbsp red rice
150g/5½oz sugar snap peas,
   sliced lengthways
150g/5½oz radishes, quartered
1 avocado, cubed
4 spring onions (scallions),
   finely sliced
50g/2oz lamb's lettuce
50g/2oz ricotta salata
salt and freshly ground
   black pepper
For the dressing
zest and juice 1 orange
2 tsp Dijon mustard
1 tbsp sherry vinegar
3 tbsp extra virgin olive oil
2 tsp agave

Cook the rice in salted water according to the packet instructions. Drain, then spread it out on a tray and leave to cool. Meanwhile, combine the ingredients for the dressing in a small bowl and season well.

In a large bowl, toss together the cooled rice, sugar snap peas, radishes, avocado, spring onions, lamb's lettuce and dressing. Taste and season, then pile onto a serving dish and shave over the ricotta salata.

MEDITERRANEAN
★
TUNA RICE SALAD

This simple salad is full of the flavours of summer: olives, rosemary and roasted vegetables. Now all you need is a glass of wine and some sunshine and you're there!

 SERVES 2

TAKES 35 minutes

85g/½ cup mixed basmati, red and wild rice
1 large sprig rosemary
120g/4oz good-quality canned tuna (drained weight)
25g/1oz mixed olives, halved
75g/2½oz roasted red (bell) peppers, roughly chopped
75g/2½oz oven-roasted or sunblushed tomatoes in oil, drained and quartered if whole (though reserve 2 tsp oil)
75g/2½oz canned sweetcorn, drained
1 large red or regular spring onion (scallion), finely sliced
50g/2oz mixed salad leaves
salt and black pepper
For the dressing
1 heaped tbsp mayonnaise
½ tsp sherry vinegar
¼ tsp very finely chopped rosemary leaves

Cook the rice in salted water according to the packet instructions, adding the sprig of rosemary to the water. Drain, then spread it out on a tray and leave to cool, discarding the rosemary sprig.

Meanwhile, make the dressing. Mix together the mayonnaise, vinegar, rosemary and 1 tbsp cold water in a small bowl. Chill until ready to serve.

Combine the tuna, olives, peppers, tomatoes, sweetcorn and spring onion in a large bowl. Stir through the cooled rice, season and add 2 tsp oil from the tomato jar. Divide the salad leaves between plates or bowls, top with the rice salad and drizzle over the dressing.

HALLOUMI & HARISSA

★

'TABBOULEH'

This Middle-Eastern dish is traditionally made with bulgur wheat, but rice works just as well in this fresh herby salad.

SERVES 3

TAKES 45 minutes

100g/½ cup plus 1 tbsp wholegrain
    jasmine rice
50g/2oz flat-leaf parsley,
    finely chopped
½ bunch mint,
    finely chopped
4 spring onions (scallions),
    finely chopped
125g/4½oz cherry tomatoes,
    finely chopped
100g/4oz cucumber,
    finely chopped
½ tsp allspice
juice ½ lemon
1 tbsp extra virgin olive oil
250g/9oz block halloumi, cut
    into 12 slices
handful pomegranate seeds
salt and freshly ground
    black pepper

For the dressing
1 heaped tbsp harissa
juice ½ lemon
2 tbsp extra virgin olive oil
1 tbsp honey

Cook the rice in salted water according to the packet instructions. Drain, then spread it out on a tray and leave to cool.

Combine the herbs, spring onions, tomatoes, cucumber, allspice, lemon juice, oil and some seasoning together in a bowl. Add the cooled rice and mix well. To make the dressing, mix together the harissa, lemon juice, oil, honey and seasoning.

Heat a non-stick frying pan over a medium heat and fry the halloumi slices in batches until golden brown and soft. Top the tabbouleh with the halloumi, drizzle over the dressing and scatter with pomegranate seeds.

RICE SLAW

Make a slaw more of a meal by adding rice. Mango chutney is an underrated ingredient, and here it is used to brighten the dressing and add depth of flavour.

SERVES 4

TAKES 50 minutes

150g/¾ cup plus 1 tbsp
   wholegrain jasmine rice
25g/½ cup coconut flakes
1 tsp nigella seeds
1 large carrot, grated
200g/7oz red cabbage, shredded
1 small red onion, finely sliced
1 small mango, sliced
2 ready-roasted chicken
   legs, shredded
handful chives, finely chopped
salt and freshly ground
   black pepper
For the dressing
3–4 tbsp mango chutney
100g/4oz Greek yoghurt
zest and juice 1 lime

Cook the rice in salted water according to the packet instructions. Drain, then spread it out on a tray and leave to cool.

Heat a small frying pan and toast the coconut flakes until golden brown, then tip into a bowl. Spoon the nigella seeds into the pan and lightly toast, then add to the coconut flakes. Combine the dressing ingredients together in a small bowl.

In a large bowl, mix together the carrot, cabbage, onion, mango, chicken and cooled rice. Stir through the dressing, taste and season, then transfer to a serving dish. Scatter over the coconut flakes, nigella seeds and chives.

Tip: To roast your own chicken legs, preheat the oven to 200°C/400°F/gas 6. Rub two chicken legs with olive oil, season and roast for 40–45 minutes, or until cooked through.

MEXICAN
★
BLACK RICE

With its firm texture, black rice is a great salad base. Add sweet tomatoes and sweetcorn, salty feta and a tangy lime dressing for a dish that's bursting with sunshine.

SERVES 4–6

TAKES 35 minutes

250g/1¼ cups black rice
2 sweetcorn cobs
250g/9oz mixed baby tomatoes
1 large red onion, finely chopped
½ small bunch mint, roughly
  chopped
½ small bunch coriander
  (cilantro), roughly chopped
½ small bunch flat-leaf parsley,
  roughly chopped
150g/5½oz feta, broken
  into chunks
salt and freshly ground
  black pepper
For the dressing
3 tbsp extra virgin olive oil
zest and juice 2 limes
1 green chilli, deseeded and
  finely chopped
2 garlic cloves, crushed

Cook the rice in salted water according to the packet instructions. Drain, then spread it out on a tray and leave to cool.

Meanwhile, bring a pan of water to the boil and cook the corn cobs for 10–15 minutes until tender. Drain and leave to cool. Mix all the dressing ingredients together in a bowl and season.

Slice the kernels from the cobs and tip them into a large bowl. Add the rice and remaining ingredients, except for the feta. Pour over the dressing and toss everything together. Divide between plates and crumble over the feta.

TOASTED RICE WITH

★

THAI PORK

Despite many variations, this Lao and Thai salad should always feature ground toasted rice. Make sure you don't cook the pork for too long – it should still be juicy. Serve with some sticky rice to make it more substantial.

 SERVES 4–6

TAKES 30 minutes, plus cooling

2½ tbsp Thai sticky rice (glutinous rice)
2 tbsp sesame oil
500g/1lb 2oz pork mince
3 banana shallots, finely chopped
2½ tbsp fish sauce
2 tsp brown sugar
zest and juice 1 lime, plus extra lime wedges to serve
½ heaped tsp chilli flakes, roughly crushed, plus extra to serve
½ small bunch Thai basil, picked leaves
½ small bunch coriander, picked (cilantro) leaves
handful mint leaves
salt and freshly ground black pepper
To serve
1 iceberg lettuce, split into leaves
¼ cucumber, quartered lengthways then sliced

Heat a large frying pan, tip in the rice and toast for 5–6 minutes until golden brown, shaking every so often. Tip the rice into a pestle and mortar or spice grinder and grind to a powder, then set aside.

Heat 1 tablespoon of the oil in the pan over a high heat. Add the pork mince and fry for 8–10 minutes until browned and just starting to caramelise – any liquid should have evaporated but the meat should still be juicy and cooked through. Turn off the heat, add the shallots to the pan and stir, then tip the mixture into a bowl.

Combine the fish sauce, remaining sesame oil, sugar and lime zest and juice in a small bowl. Add this to the pork whilst still warm along with the chilli flakes and half the ground rice, and leave to cool. Stir through most of the herbs, taste and season. Serve the mince with a pile of lettuce leaves and bowls of the cucumber slices, remaining herbs, ground rice, chilli flakes and lime wedges, and let everyone help themselves.

ROASTED VEGETABLE
★
PESTO RICE

The pesto dressing doesn't include cheese, so if you want
to make this salad vegan, just leave out the Parmesan
shavings at the end.

SERVES 6

TAKES 50 minutes

1 large courgette (zucchini), sliced
   into 5mm/¼in rounds
1 red onion, cut into wedges
1 aubergine (eggplant), cut into
   1.5cm/½in cubes
2 (bell) peppers (red or yellow, or
   a mix), cut into chunks
2½ tbsp extra virgin olive oil
250g/1⅓ cups wild rice
100g/3½oz spinach, roughly sliced
25g/1oz Parmesan shavings
salt and freshly ground
   black pepper
For the pesto
50g/2oz almonds
50g/2oz basil leaves
1 garlic clove, crushed
3 tbsp extra virgin olive oil
zest ½ lemon and a squeeze
   of juice

Preheat the oven to 200°C/400°F/gas 6. Toss the
courgette, onion, aubergine and red and yellow
peppers in 2½ tbsp oil with some seasoning. Tip
onto parchment-lined baking trays, spreading out
to a single layer. Roast for 35 – 45 minutes until
golden and beginning to caramelise.

Meanwhile, cook the rice according to the packet
instructions. Drain, then spread it out on a tray and
leave to cool.

To make the pesto, toast the almonds in the oven
for 5–8 minutes until golden, then tip them into
the small bowl of a food processor. Add the basil,
garlic, 3 tbsp oil, plenty of seasoning and 4 –5 tbsp
water, and the lemon zest and juice. Blitz until
smooth. Stir 5 tbsp of the dressing through the
rice, along with the spinach. Taste and season,
then arrange on a serving plate. Spoon over the
vegetables and drizzle over the remaining dressing.
Top with Parmesan shavings and grind over some
black pepper.

COCONUT RICE &

★

THAI BEEF

Using coconut milk (the drinking variety) gives this rice all the coconut flavour but without the calories or heaviness of using the full-fat canned variety.

SERVES 2

TAKES 40 minutes

100g/½ cup plus 1 tbsp
   jasmine rice
200ml/7fl oz coconut milk from a
   carton (not full-fat from a can)
2 tbsp rice vinegar
2 tsp caster (granulated) sugar
¼ tsp salt
1 small red onion, thinly sliced
1 x 250g/9oz bavette steak
drizzle of sunflower oil
½ small bunch Thai basil,
   roughly torn
large handful coriander (cilantro)
   leaves, roughly torn
salt and freshly ground pepper
For the dressing
1 tbsp fish sauce
2 tbsp onion pickling liquid
1–2 red bird's eye chillies,
   deseeded and finely chopped
1 garlic clove, crushed
juice ½ lime
pinch of sugar

Tip the rice into a saucepan with some salt and pour over the coconut milk. Bring to the boil, then reduce the heat, cover and simmer for 15 minutes. Turn off the heat and leave to steam for 10 minutes.

Meanwhile, combine the vinegar, sugar, salt and 2 tbsp cold water in a small bowl. Add the onion and set aside to pickle.

Rub the steak with a little oil and season. Heat a griddle or frying pan over a high heat. Once hot, cook the steak for 1½–2 minutes on each side, depending on the thickness – you want it to be pink in the middle. Set aside to rest.

Fork through the cooked rice, then tip it onto a tray and allow it to cool. Drain the pickled onion, reserving 2 tbsp of the liquid. Combine the ingredients for the dressing in a small bowl. Gently toss together the rice, dressing, herbs, and half the pickled onion. Divide between plates then top with the remaining onion.

AUBERGINE, TARRAGON &
★
POMEGRANATE SALAD

Dress the salad whilst warm so that the aubergines and
rice have the opportunity to soak up the dressing.
The pomegranate molasses adds a sweet-and-sourness
to balance the oil.

SERVES 4

TAKES 45 minutes

250g/1¼ cups wholegrain
  basmati rice
2 large aubergines (eggplants),
  cut into 1.5cm/½in wedges
2 tbsp extra virgin olive oil
25g/1oz pine nuts, toasted
50g/2oz rocket (arugula)
½ small bunch tarragon,
  finely chopped
25g/1oz crispy onions,
  from a packet
salt and freshly ground
  black pepper

For the dressing
2½ tbsp extra virgin olive oil
1 garlic clove, crushed
zest 1 lemon and 2 tbsp juice
2 tbsp pomegranate molasses

Cook the rice in salted water according to the
packet instructions. Meanwhile, preheat the oven
to 200°C/400°F/gas 6. Mix the aubergines with the
oil and some seasoning in a bowl. Tip onto two
parchment-lined trays and roast for 25–30 minutes.
Combine the dressing ingredients together in a
small bowl and season.

Tip the rice and aubergines into a bowl, then pour
over the dressing whilst still warm. Mix well and
leave to cool to room temperature. Stir through
the pine nuts, rocket, tarragon and some seasoning,
then scatter over the crispy onions before serving.

SOUPS &

★

SNACKS

FONTINA, PROSCIUTTO & ★ SAGE ARANCINI

Meaning 'little oranges', these delightful snacks originated in Sicily but can now be found all over Italy. Different regions have their own takes on the recipe, but traditionally, the centre would have been filled with ragù. The highlight of this version is the oozing cheese centre.

 MAKES 12 large arancini

TAKES about 1 hour, plus chilling

pinch saffron
750ml/1½ pints hot
    vegetable stock
25g/1oz butter
250g/1¼ cups arborio rice
50g/2oz Parmesan, finely grated
zest ½ lemon, finely grated
10 large sage leaves, finely
    chopped
vegetable oil, for deep frying
salt

For the filling
75g/2½oz fontina, cut into
    12 pieces
3 slices prosciutto ham,
    torn into 12 pieces

For the coating
3 tbsp seasoned plain
    (all-purpose) flour
2 eggs, beaten
85g/3oz panko breadcrumbs

Steep the saffron in the stock for 10 minutes. Melt the butter in a saucepan, add the rice and ½ tsp salt and stir to coat. Pour over 500ml/17fl oz of the infused stock and bring to a simmer. Cook for 18–20 minutes, stirring, until the stock has been absorbed and the rice is al dente. Add more stock if needed. Scatter over the Parmesan and lemon zest and leave for a few moments, then add the sage and stir well. Tip onto a tray, spread out and leave to cool, then chill until firm.

Divide the rice into 12 equal portions and shape into balls. Make a hole in the centre of each ball with your index finger and stuff in a piece of fontina and prosciutto, then reshape into a ball. Coat the balls in the seasoned flour, followed by the beaten egg and finally the breadcrumbs.

Half-fill a large saucepan with oil and heat to 170°C/340°F/gas 4. Cook the balls in batches for 6–8 minutes, turning frequently and making sure the oil comes back up to temperature between batches. Drain on kitchen paper, sprinkle with salt and leave to cool a little before eating.

ITALIAN MEATBALL &
★
RICE BROTH

Hearty and warming just like mamma used to make, this
Italian-inspired soup is so quick and easy to put together.
Even after the hardest day, a bowlful of this broth will
make it all better.

SERVES 4

TAKES 35 minutes

250g/9oz beef mince
1 large garlic clove, crushed
50g/2oz Parmesan, finely grated,
    plus extra to serve
35g/1¼oz fresh breadcrumbs
1 egg, beaten
handful parsley, finely chopped,
    plus extra to serve
1.5 litres/3 pints fresh beef stock
125g/scant ¾ cup carnaroli rice
150g/5½oz cavolo nero or kale,
    tough stalks removed and
    roughly sliced
125g/4½oz frozen peas
salt and freshly ground
    black pepper

Combine the beef mince, garlic, Parmesan,
breadcrumbs, egg, parsley and seasoning in a bowl.
Shape the mixture into tiny meatballs about the
size of a small cherry tomato.

Tip the stock into a saucepan and bring to the boil,
add the rice and simmer for 5 minutes, then drop
in the meatballs. Bring back to a gentle simmer and
cook for 10 minutes. Add the cavolo nero and peas
and cook for a further 5 minutes. Taste and season,
then ladle into bowls and grate over some extra
Parmesan before serving.

CHEESY

★

RICE FRITTERS

These cheesy fritters are great for using up leftover rice.
Jazz them up by adding whatever you fancy: a handful
of chopped chives, tarragon, caraway seeds, olives,
sunblushed tomatoes or capers. They're great with
mango chutney or a dollop of ketchup, too.

MAKES 12–16 fritters

TAKES 50 minutes

150g/¾ cup long-grain rice
  (white or wholegrain)
1 onion, coarsely grated
100g/3½oz mature Cheddar, grated
50g/generous ⅓ cup plain
  (all-purpose) flour
¼ whole nutmeg, freshly grated
2 eggs
2 tsp Dijon mustard
5 tbsp milk
2–3 tbsp sunflower oil
salt and freshly ground
  black pepper
sweet tomato and chilli chutney,
  to serve

Cook the rice in salted water according to the
packet instructions. Drain, then spread it out on
a tray and leave to cool.

Tip the rice into a large bowl and add the onion,
Cheddar, flour, nutmeg and plenty of seasoning.
In a separate bowl beat together the eggs,
mustard and milk, then pour over the rice
and stir to combine.

Heat 1 tbsp of the oil in a large non-stick frying
pan over a medium–high heat. Spoon heaped
tablespoons of the mixture into the pan and
spread out a little using the back of the spoon.
Fry for about 3 minutes on each side until golden
brown, then transfer to a plate lined with kitchen
paper. Add a little more oil to the pan and continue
with the remaining batter. Serve with a tomato
and chilli chutney.

RICE

★

PAKORAS

Everything tastes good deep-fried, and when flavoured
with heady spices, fresh coriander and red onion, rice
is elevated to a new level. Adjust the quantity of chillies
depending on how much heat you can handle.

 MAKES about 20 pakoras

TAKES 45 minutes

75g/⅓ cup basmati and wild rice
2 red onions, sliced
1 green chilli, deseeded and
   finely chopped
2cm/¾in piece of ginger, peeled
   and finely grated
100g/generous ¾ cup gram flour
1 tsp ground turmeric
2 tsp garam masala
1 tsp cumin seeds
½ small bunch coriander
   (cilantro), roughly chopped
vegetable oil, for deep frying
salt
chutney and raita, to serve

Cook the rice in salted water according to the
packet instructions. Leave to cool a little, then
lightly mash in the pan. Tip the onions, chilli, ginger,
flour and spices into a large bowl with plenty of
salt. Add the cooled rice and enough cold water
(about 85ml/2¾fl oz) to make a thick paste. Stir
through the coriander.

Half-fill a deep saucepan with oil and heat to
180°C/355°F/gas 4. Drop spoonfuls of the mixture
into the hot oil and fry for about 3 minutes until
crisp and golden. Drain on kitchen paper, sprinkle
with salt, then continue with the remaining
batter. Serve immediately with chutney and
raita for dipping.

SPICED

PUFFED RICE

Like a far superior version of Bombay mix, this moreish snack would traditionally be served with tea like chai masala. Get the ingredients ready and weighed out before you start cooking.

SERVES 6–8 as a snack

TAKES 15 minutes

1 heaped tbsp coconut oil
1½ tsp black mustard seeds
1 tsp fennel seeds
50g/2oz peanuts, skin on
4 garlic cloves, peeled and bashed
15 fresh curry leaves
25g/1oz pumpkin seeds
¾ tsp turmeric
¼–½ tsp hot chilli powder
⅛ tsp asafoetida
¾ tsp salt
50g/2oz raisins (use golden raisins if you can)
50g/1 cup coconut flakes
75g/2½ cups puffed brown rice

Heat the oil in a wok over a medium–high heat. Add the mustard seeds, fennel seeds, peanuts and garlic and cook for 1–2 minutes, stirring until golden. Throw in the curry leaves and pumpkin seeds and let them sizzle until the pumpkin seeds start to pop. Add the spices and salt and stir for a few seconds, then tip in the raisins and coconut flakes and stir for a further 1 minute, or until browned.

Turn down the heat and add the puffed rice. Stir to coat well, then transfer to a bowl and allow to cool. Keep for up to one week in an airtight container.

SUMMER

★

ROLLS

Swapping the traditional rice noodles for rice in these Vietnamese summer rolls really works. They're bright and fresh with plenty of herbs, and a sprinkling of peanuts adds some crunch.

MAKES 6 large rolls

TAKES 45 minutes

100g/generous ½ cup sushi rice
6 Vietnamese rice papers
    (22cm/9in in diameter)
1 avocado, peeled and thinly sliced
150g/5½oz (about 18) cooked
    king prawns (shrimp)
large handful each coriander
    (cilantro) leaves, mint leaves
    and Thai basil leaves
1 little gem lettuce, split
    into leaves
25g/1oz salted and roasted
    peanuts, roughly crushed
salt
For the dipping sauce
3 tbsp hoisin sauce
2 tbsp sweet chilli sauce
1 tbsp rice wine vinegar

Cook the rice in salted water according to the packet instructions. Drain, then spread it out on a tray and leave to cool. Using wet hands, divide the rice into six equal portions and shape into logs.

Fill a large frying pan with warm water. Soak a rice paper in the warm water until softened, then transfer it to a chopping board. Fan some slices of avocado over the centre of the rice paper, top with three prawns, a log of rice, some herbs and a lettuce leaf or two. Sprinkle over some crushed peanuts.

Fold in the sides, then tightly roll up the rice paper to enclose the filling. Repeat with the remaining rice papers and ingredients, changing the order of the filling if you wish.

In a small bowl, combine the ingredients for the dipping sauce, top with the remaining crushed peanuts and serve with the summer rolls.

SRIRACHA MAYO &
★
CHICKEN ONIGIRAZU

The Japanese can't get enough of these seaweed and rice
'sandwiches'. Fill them with anything you fancy –
the combinations are endless.

MAKES 2 sandwiches

TAKES 50 minutes

125g/scant ¾ cup sushi rice
2 tbsp rice wine vinegar
½ tsp caster (granulated) sugar
4 radishes, thinly sliced
1 tsp Sriracha chilli sauce
2½ heaped tbsp mayonnaise
4 sheets of nori
2 handfuls rocket (arugula)
100g/3½oz cooked chicken
   breast slices
salt

Wash the rice thoroughly, then tip it into a saucepan
with some salt and pour over 165ml/5½fl oz boiling
water. Bring to the boil, then cover and simmer over
the lowest heat for 15 minutes. Set aside, covered,
for 10 minutes, then leave to cool completely.

Meanwhile, mix together the vinegar, sugar and
2 tbsp cold water with a little salt in a small bowl.
Stir in the radishes and set aside. In a separate small
bowl, combine the chilli sauce and mayonnaise.

Lay a piece of clingfilm on your work surface. Top
with two sheets of nori, shiny-side down, so that
they just overlap. Wet the inside of a small bowl
with water, then pack one-quarter of the rice into
the bowl, then turn out into the centre of the
nori. Top the rice with one-quarter of the sauce,
some drained radishes, a handful of rocket, half the
chicken and another spoonful of the sauce. Top all
this with another one-quarter of the rice, shaped in
the same way. Trim the edges of the nori if you have
lots of excess, then lightly dampen the edges. Using
the clingfilm, pull the nori up and over the filling to
enclose it. Wrap tightly in the clingfilm to form a
square. Chill for 15 minutes. Repeat with remaining
ingredients to make another sandwich. Unwrap and
use a hot knife to slice them in half.

STUFFED

★

VINE LEAVES

A staple of the mezze table throughout the Middle East, Turkey and Greece, these little parcels of joy are easy to make and the yield is high, although they won't last long.

Makes about 30–40 stuffed leaves

TAKES 2 hours

250g/9oz vine leaves in brine (drained weight)
200g/1 cup plus 2 tbsp long-grain rice
6 tbsp extra virgin olive oil
50g/2oz pine nuts
2 large onions, finely chopped
4 garlic cloves, crushed
¾ tsp allspice
50g/2oz currants
zest 1 lemon and juice ½ lemon
2 tsp dried mint
½ small bunch dill, finely chopped
500ml/17fl oz hot vegetable stock
salt and freshly ground black pepper
Greek yoghurt and lemon wedges, to serve

Soak the vine leaves in just-boiled water for 20 minutes, then drain and pat dry with kitchen paper. Soak the rice in water for 10 minutes.

Heat 1 tbsp of the oil in a frying pan, add the pine nuts and fry until golden, then remove using a slotted spoon. Keep the pan on the heat and add another 1 tbsp oil. Tip in the onions and cook for 8–10 minutes until softened. Stir in the garlic and allspice and cook for 2 minutes. Drain the rice, add it to the pan and fry for 1 minute, coating it in the oil. Remove from the heat and stir through the pine nuts, currants, lemon zest and juice, herbs, plenty of seasoning and 1 tbsp oil. Spoon 1–2 heaped tsp onto a vine leaf, then fold in the sides and roll up. Repeat the process with the remaining mixture. You should have vine leaves left over.

Line the bottom of a large saucepan with half the unfilled leaves, then arrange the filled parcels snugly on top in layers. Pour over the stock and remaining oil then cover with the remaining leaves. Sit a plate on top to press the leaves down. Bring to a simmer, cover and cook for 50 minutes–1 hour until the water has been absorbed and the rice is cooked. Remove from the heat and leave to steam with the lid on for 10 minutes, then remove the lid and leave to cool. Serve with yoghurt and lemon wedges.

MULLIGATAWNY
★
SOUP

There are lots of variations on this curried soup – an anglicised recipe that became popular when the British were in India during colonial times.

SERVES 6–8

TAKES about 1 hour

2 tbsp sunflower oil
1 large onion, finely chopped
1 carrot, finely chopped
2 sticks celery, finely chopped
3 garlic cloves, crushed
4-cm/1⅝-in piece of ginger, peeled and finely chopped
2 tsp garam masala
½ tsp turmeric
1½ tbsp curry powder
½ nutmeg, finely grated
125g/¾ cup dried red lentils
550g/1lb 3oz peeled and chopped butternut squash
2 tbsp tomato purée
1.2 litres/2½ pints vegetable stock
400ml/14fl oz can coconut milk
175g/1 cup jasmine rice
salt and black pepper

For the topping
1 green apple, cut into matchsticks
juice ½ lime, plus lime wedges to serve
50g/2oz cashew nuts, toasted
handful coriander (cilantro) leaves

Heat the oil in a large saucepan over a medium heat. Add the onion, carrot and celery and cook for about 8 minutes until softened. Stir through the garlic, ginger and spices and cook for 2 minutes more. Tip in the lentils, butternut squash and tomato purée and stir together. Pour over the stock and coconut milk, then bring to a simmer. Cover and cook for 30 minutes until the lentils and squash are soft. Leave to cool a little.

Meanwhile, cook the rice according to the packet instructions. Blend the soup in batches together with half of the rice until smooth. Tip back into the pan, then stir through the remaining unblended rice, adding a little more water if too thick. Season and warm through.

Mix together the apple matchsticks and lime juice. Ladle the soup into bowls, top with the apple, cashew nuts and a few coriander leaves. Serve extra lime wedges on the side for squeezing over.

AVGOLEMONO
★
SOUP

Light and refreshing, this classic Greek soup is often served at Christmas time. It's thickened with egg, and the rice helps to emulsify everything. It has a lovely velvety texture.

🍴 SERVES 6

⏰ TAKES 45 minutes

1.5 litres/3 pints fresh chicken
    stock
3 chicken breasts
125g/scant ¾ cup long-grain rice
6 eggs
juice 2 lemons and zest 1 lemon
large knob butter
handful dill, finely chopped
salt and freshly ground
    black pepper

Bring the stock to the boil in a large saucepan. Turn the heat down to a gentle simmer, add the chicken and poach for 10–15 minutes, or until cooked through – cut through the thickest part of the largest breast to check. Remove using a slotted spoon and set aside to cool. Bring the stock back to the boil, add the rice and simmer for 12 minutes, then turn off the heat.

Whisk the eggs in a bowl for 2 minutes until light and frothy. Add the lemon juice, 1 tsp lemon zest and some seasoning, then whisk in 200ml/7fl oz of the hot stock from the rice pan. Slowly pour the egg mixture into the pan of rice and stock, stirring all the time. Gently simmer for about 10 minutes, continuing to stir, until the soup has amalgamated and thickened a little. Be careful it doesn't boil as the eggs will scramble. Shred the chicken and stir it into the soup with the butter. Taste and season.

Ladle into bowls, scatter over the dill, remaining lemon zest and grind over some black pepper.

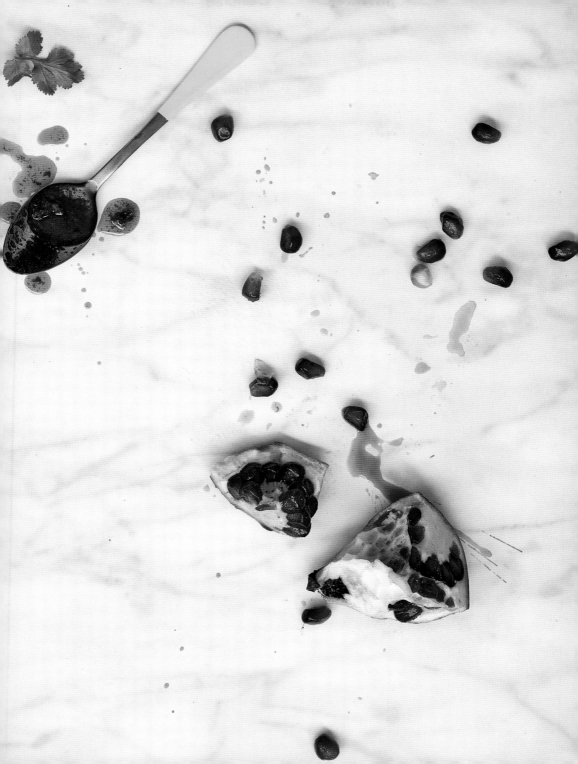

RISI E

★

BISI

This dish should be like a risotto, but a little more soupy. You should still be able to eat it with a fork – adjust the quantity of liquid if needed. Leave out the pancetta and Parmesan and use vegetable stock to make it veggie.

SERVES 4

TAKES 40 minutes

25g/1oz butter
2 tsp olive oil
1 onion, finely chopped
2 garlic cloves, crushed
225g/1¼ cups arborio or
   carnaroli rice
small bunch parsley, finely
   chopped
1.2 litres/2½ pints hot chicken
   or vegetable stock
375g/13oz frozen peas
50g/2oz Parmesan
12 thin slices pancetta
handful pea shoots (optional)
salt and freshly ground
   black pepper

Melt the butter and 1 tsp of the oil in a saucepan. Fry the onion for 8 minutes until softened, then stir in the garlic. Add the rice and half the parsley and stir to coat. Pour over the stock, season, bring to a simmer and cook for 15 minutes, stirring now and then.

Add the peas and cook for 5 minutes more, or until the rice is al dente. Turn off the heat and stir through the Parmesan and some seasoning.

Meanwhile, heat the remaining oil in a frying pan and fry the pancetta until crispy. Spoon the rice into shallow bowls, top with the crispy pancetta and oil from the pan, then scatter over the remaining parsley and the pea shoots (if using).

YAKI

★

ONIGIRI

Crispy on the outside and soft on the inside, these rice triangles are a popular Japanese snack. 'Yaki' means grilled, and they were originally a food of the samurai, who took them to battle and then grilled them in a fire, charring the outside. The miso glaze gives an umami hit.

 SERVES 6

TAKES 1 hour

250g/1¼ cups sushi rice
1 tsp miso paste
2 tbsp soy sauce
1 tbsp toasted sesame oil
1 tsp honey
2 tbsp sesame seeds (mixture of
  black and white)
salt
pickled ginger and sliced spring
  onions (scallions), to serve

Wash the rice thoroughly, then tip it into a saucepan with some salt and pour over 330ml/11fl oz boiling water. Bring to the boil, then cover and simmer over the lowest heat for 15 minutes. Set aside, covered, for 10 minutes, then leave to cool completely.

Mix together the miso, soy sauce, ½ tsp of the sesame oil and the honey in a small bowl until smooth. Stir the sesame seeds through the cooled rice. Using wet hands, divide the rice into six equal portions and shape into triangles or circles about 6–7cm/3in wide and 2.5cm/1in thick.

Heat a large non-stick frying pan over a medium heat and drizzle in the remaining sesame oil. Fry the onigiri on one side for 8–10 minutes until starting to brown and crisp. Carefully turn over and brush the toasted side with the soy mix. Continue to fry until the other side is browned and crisp. Turn off the heat. One at a time flip over the onigiri and brush with the mix, then quickly transfer to a plate. Brush over any remaining soy mix. Leave to cool a little, then serve with pickled ginger and a sprinkling of spring onions.

SMOKED HADDOCK
★
KEDGEREE

It's not clear how kedgeree came to be, but one theory is that it's a colonial version of the South-Asian dish khichri, dating back to the 1300s. Wherever it comes from, it makes a cracking supper or brunch.

🍴 SERVES 4

⏰ TAKES about 1 hour

300g/10½oz skinless and boneless smoked undyed haddock
1 bay leaf
good grating fresh nutmeg
600ml/1¼ pints whole milk
50g/2oz butter
1 onion, finely chopped
2 tsp curry powder
1 tsp turmeric
3 cardamom pods, lightly bashed
280g/1½ cups basmati rice
4 eggs
½ small bunch chives, finely chopped
½ small bunch coriander (cilantro), roughly chopped
salt and freshly ground black pepper
1 lemon, cut into wedges, to serve

Place the haddock in a saucepan, and add the bay leaf, nutmeg and some black pepper. Pour over the milk – the fish should be just covered, so add more milk if needed. Bring to a simmer, then turn off the heat, cover and set aside for 10 minutes.

Remove the fish from the milk and set aside, discard the bay leaf but keep the milk. Rinse the pan and return it to the heat, add half the butter and gently fry the onion for 8 minutes. Add the spices and stir, then add the rice and some salt and stir to coat. Pour over the reserved milk, bring to the boil, then cover and simmer gently for 15 minutes. Turn off the heat, dot over the remaining butter and lay the fish on top, then cover and set aside for 10 minutes.

Bring a small pan of water to the boil, lower in the eggs and simmer for 6½ minutes, then run under cold water. Peel, halve and quarter them. Gently fork the fish through the rice and stir through most of the chives and coriander. Divide between plates and top with the egg quarters. Scatter over the remaining herbs and serve with lemon wedges.

STUFFED

★

PEPPERS

A classic recipe, these peppers are proper comfort food.
Any leftovers are great served cold the next day.

🍴 SERVES 6

⏰ TAKES about 1 hour
30 minutes

2 tbsp extra virgin olive oil, plus
   extra for drizzling
1 onion, finely chopped
2 large garlic cloves, crushed
150g/¾ cup easy-cook
   long-grain rice
600ml/1¼ pints hot lamb or
   beef stock
6 mixed colour (bell) peppers
2 tsp allspice
250g/9oz lamb mince
50g/2oz pine nuts, toasted
2 tbsp tomato purée
50g/2oz raisins
1 small bunch parsley,
   finely chopped
1 tsp salt
freshly ground black pepper
For the yoghurt
250g/9oz Greek yoghurt
1 garlic clove, crushed
handful dill, finely chopped

Preheat the oven to 200°C/400°F/gas 6. Heat the oil in a frying pan and cook the onion for about 8 minutes until softened. Add the garlic and rice and stir. Turn the heat down and pour in 150ml/5fl oz of the stock. Cover and simmer for 10 minutes until all the water has been absorbed. Tip into a large bowl and leave to cool.

Slice the tops from the peppers, reserving the lids, and scoop out the seeds and core. Place in a casserole dish – trim the bottoms without making any holes to make them stand, if needed.

Add the allspice, lamb mince, pine nuts, tomato purée, raisins and parsley to the cooled rice, along with 150ml/5fl oz of the stock, the salt and some black pepper. Spoon into the peppers, packing the mixture down. Pour over a little of the stock, then pop the pepper lids back on. Drizzle generously with oil and pour the remaining stock into the bottom of the dish. Cover with foil and bake for 45 minutes. Remove the foil and bake for a further 20 minutes.

Meanwhile, mix together the yoghurt, garlic, dill and some seasoning and serve alongside the peppers.

CHILLI BUTTER

★

SPRING GREEN PILAF

Use frozen baby broad beans to make this quicker. If using older beans, you'll need to double pod them as the skins will be too tough to eat.

SERVES 4

TAKES 40 minutes

280g/1½ cups basmati rice
75g/2½oz butter
2 leeks, thinly sliced
2 garlic cloves, crushed
½ tsp allspice
425ml/15fl oz hot vegetable or
    chicken stock
300g/10½oz podded baby broad
    beans, defrosted if frozen
250g/9oz bunch asparagus, sliced
    into 4cm/1½in pieces
50g/2oz pistachios, roughly
    chopped
½ small bunch dill, finely chopped
salt and freshly ground
    black pepper
To serve
Greek yoghurt
1½–2 tsp Aleppo chilli flakes

Tip the rice into a bowl and cover with cold water. Meanwhile, heat 50g/2oz of the butter in a large saucepan over a medium heat. Once foaming, add the leeks and cook for 8 minutes until softened. Stir through the garlic and allspice. Drain the rice, add it to the pan and stir to coat in the butter. Pour over the stock, season and bring to the boil, then reduce the heat to its lowest setting, cover and simmer for 10 minutes.

Quickly lift the lid and scatter over the broad beans and asparagus, cover and cook for a further 5 minutes. Remove from the heat and set aside to steam for 10 minutes.

Toast the pistachios in a frying pan. Stir the dill and pistachios into the rice. Divide between plates and top with a dollop of Greek yoghurt. Return the frying pan to the heat and add the final 25g/1oz butter. Once foaming, add the chilli flakes, sizzle for a moment, then pour a little over each plate.

MUSHROOM, MASCARPONE &
TRUFFLE RISOTTO

Posh up a traditional mushroom risotto with some
fancy mushrooms, truffle oil and rich, creamy, cooling
mascarpone. Make sure the rice still has a firm centre
when you turn off the heat, as it will soften further
when resting.

SERVES 2

TAKES 45 minutes,
plus soaking

15g/½oz dried porcini mushrooms
25g/1oz butter
1 small onion, finely chopped
175g/1 cup arborio rice
100ml/3½fl oz white wine
500–600ml/17fl oz–1¼ pints hot
   vegetable or chicken stock
225g/8oz mixed mushrooms,
   sliced
1 tbsp tarragon, finely chopped
25g/1oz Parmesan, finely grated
2 tbsp mascarpone
drizzle truffle oil
salt and freshly ground
   black pepper

Soak the porcini in 150ml/5fl oz boiling water for
30 minutes. Drain, reserving the mushroom liquid,
and roughly chop.

Melt half the butter in a saucepan over a medium
heat. Add the onion and cook for 5–8 minutes
until softened. Stir through the rice and toast for
2 minutes. Pour in the wine and let it bubble,
stirring until evaporated. Add the porcini and its
soaking liquid and stir until absorbed.

Add the stock a ladleful at a time, stirring and
letting the rice absorb most of the liquid before
adding some more. This will take about 20 minutes.
Stop when the rice is al dente then turn off the
heat – you may not need to use all of the stock.

Heat the remaining butter in a large frying pan
and fry the mixed mushrooms until golden brown,
then season. Stir half the mushrooms through the
risotto, along with 2 tsp of the tarragon. Scatter
over the Parmesan, cover and leave for 5 minutes.
Gently stir the risotto, then divide between bowls,
top with the remaining mushrooms, a dollop of
mascarpone, a drizzle of truffle oil, the remaining
tarragon and a grinding of black pepper.

BULGOGI

★

BIBIMBAP

There are lots of components in this dish, but it can come together quickly if you have everything chopped, sliced and ready to go before you start cooking.

SERVES 2

TAKES about 1 hour

250g/9oz sirloin steak, fat
   removed and thinly sliced
4 radishes, sliced
200g/1 cup, plus 2 tbsp sushi rice
75g/2½oz shiitake mushrooms,
   sliced
1 garlic clove, crushed
2 tsp sesame seeds
75g/2½oz spinach
50g/2oz cucumber, quartered
   and sliced
1 small carrot, peeled and
   shredded
50g/2oz beansprouts
2 eggs
salt and freshly ground
   black pepper
Gochujang paste or Sriracha
   chilli sauce, to serve

In a bowl, mix together the marinade ingredients. Add the beef to the marinade, stir well and chill for 30 minutes. In a small bowl, mix together 2 tbsp rice vinegar, ½ tbsp honey, 2 tbsp cold water and a little salt. Add the radishes and set aside to pickle. Cook the rice according to the packet instructions, then leave to steam in a pan with the lid on.

Heat 1 tsp sesame oil in a frying pan and fry the mushrooms for 5 minutes until golden brown. Add the garlic and seasoning and fry for another 30 seconds. Remove from the pan and set aside. Heat another 1 tsp sesame oil in the pan and fry the sesame seeds until golden. Stir through the spinach until wilted, then tip into a bowl and toss with a little soy sauce and some sesame oil.

Bring a small pan of water to the boil and blanch the cucumber for 1–2 minutes until softened. Remove using a slotted spoon, transfer to a bowl and toss with some soy sauce and sesame oil. Repeat with the carrot and beansprouts.

ingredients and method continue overleaf...

★ ★ ★ ★ ★ ★ ★ ★ ★ ★ ★ ★ ★ ★ ★ ★

BULGOGI BIBIMBAP
continued...

For the marinade

1½ tbsp rice wine vinegar, plus
  extra for pickling
1 tbsp clear honey, plus extra
  for pickling
1 tsp sesame oil, plus extra for
  frying and seasoning
1½ tbsp soy sauce, plus extra
  for seasoning
2 tsp freshly grated ginger

Return the frying pan to a very high heat, drizzle in some oil, then add the beef and stir-fry for 3–4 minutes until caramelised – do this in batches so that the meat doesn't boil. Return all the beef to the pan and cook until browned and glossy. Set aside and clean out the pan. Heat a drizzle of oil in the pan and fry the eggs.

Divide the rice between wide, shallow bowls. Top with the fried eggs, then arrange the vegetables and beef over the top in separate piles so they are clearly defined. Dollop a little Gochujang on top and serve extra on the side.

SALMON

★

COULIBIAC

These individual servings of this classic Russian fish pie can be made ahead and chilled, or frozen, until ready to cook.

MAKES 4 pies

TAKES about 1 hour, plus chilling

25g/1oz butter, plus an extra knob
1 onion, finely chopped
1 garlic clove, crushed
100g/3½oz chestnut (cremini) mushrooms, finely chopped
2 salmon fillets (about 140g/ 5oz each)
85g/½ cup mixed basmati and wild rice
2 eggs, plus 1 beaten egg
½ small bunch dill, finely chopped
zest 1 lemon and juice ½ lemon
500g/1lb 2oz block all-butter puff pastry
plain (all-purpose) flour, for dusting
salt and freshly ground black pepper

Heat the 25g/1oz butter in a frying pan and soften the onion for 8 minutes. Add the garlic and mushrooms, turn up the heat and cook until golden and any liquid has evaporated. Tip into a bowl. Return the pan to the heat. Add the knob of butter, then cook the salmon, skin-side down, for 5 minutes. Flip over and remove the pan from the heat. Set aside for 3 minutes, then remove the salmon and leave to cool – it shouldn't be cooked through. Flake the fish and discard the skin.

Return the pan to the heat, add the rice and some salt, then pour over enough boiling water so that the rice is just covered. Bring to the boil, turn down the heat, cover and cook for 15 minutes. Turn off the heat and steam for 10 minutes. Drain, then spread the rice out on a tray and leave to cool.

Bring a small pan of water to the boil and cook the whole eggs for 8 minutes, then drain and run under cold water. Once cool, peel and slice them.

ingredients and method continue overleaf...

★ ★ ★ ★ ★ ★ ★ ★ ★ ★ ★ ★ ★ ★ ★ ★

★ ★

SALMON COULIBIAC

continued...

For the sauce
200g/7oz crème fraîche
1 tbsp wholegrain mustard
1 heaped tsp chopped dill

To make the sauce, warm the crème fraîche in a small saucepan and stir through the mustard, dill and a little seasoning.

Tip the rice into the mushroom and onion bowl and stir through the dill, lemon zest and juice and a little seasoning.

Line a tray with parchment paper. Roll out half the pastry on a lightly floured surface to a 28cm/11in square. Cut into four equal squares and place on the prepared tray. Spoon 4 tbsp of the rice mixture onto each square, leaving a border around the edges, then top with the salmon, eggs, remaining rice and 2 tsp of the sauce. Roll out the remaining pastry to a 30cm/12in square and cut into four equal squares. Brush the borders of the filled squares with the beaten egg and top with the pastry lids. Seal the edges, trim to neaten and crimp the edges with the tines of a fork. Use a sharp knife to poke a few air holes in the tops of the pies, brush with a little more beaten egg and chill for 30 minutes.

Preheat the oven to 200°C/400°F/gas 6. Bake the pies for 30–35 minutes and rewarm the sauce to serve alongside the pies.

SUPPER

★

DISHES

CONGEE &

★

CRISPY FIVE-SPICE TOFU

Prepared all over Asia, congee is a popular breakfast or late-supper dish. This version makes a great comforting vegetarian main, with the crispy tofu, spring onions and sesame seeds adding crunch to the soft, soothing rice.

🍴 SERVES 2

⏰ TAKES 50 minutes

175g/generous ¾ cup sushi rice
1.2 litres/2½ pints vegetable or
   chicken stock
2 cloves garlic, finely grated
5cm/2in piece of ginger, peeled
   and finely grated
175g/6oz firm tofu
1 tsp Chinese five-spice powder
sunflower oil, for frying
1 tbsp cornflour (cornstarch)
salt
To garnish
2 spring onions (scallions), white
   sliced, green shredded
2 tsp sesame seeds, toasted
soy sauce

Wash the rice thoroughly. Tip the stock, garlic and ginger into a large saucepan and bring to the boil. Add the rice, bring back to the boil, then turn down the heat and simmer for 40 minutes, stirring occasionally. When cooked, the rice should be thick and porridge-like – add more water if needed.

Meanwhile, cut the tofu into 1.5–2cm/¾in cubes, pat dry with kitchen paper and toss with the Chinese five-spice and some salt. Set aside for 30 minutes.

Heat a shallow layer of sunflower oil in a frying pan over a high heat. Toss the tofu in the cornflour and fry in the hot oil for about 5 minutes until crispy all over. Ladle the congee into bowls, top with the tofu and garnish with the spring onions, sesame seeds and some soy sauce.

NASI

★

GORENG

Meaning 'fried rice' in Indonesian. If you want to add
some prawns, after cooking the ginger and garlic stir-fry
150g/5½oz prawns until pink, then continue.

SERVES 2–3

TAKES 35 minutes

150g/¾ cup easy-cook long-grain
   wholegrain rice
3 tbsp vegetable oil
5 spring onions (scallions),
   thinly sliced
3 garlic cloves, finely chopped
2½cm/1in piece of ginger, peeled
   and shredded
2 carrots, julienned
200g/7oz Chinese cabbage,
   thickly shredded
1 tsp Asian chilli sauce, plus
   extra to serve
2 tsp tomato purée
1 tbsp soy sauce
1 tbsp kecap manis or thick sweet
   soy sauce
75g/2½oz frozen edamame beans
½ small bunch coriander
   (cilantro), roughly chopped
To garnish
2–3 eggs
handful roasted and salted
   peanuts, roughly chopped

Cook the rice according to the packet instructions.
Heat 2 tbsp of the oil in a wok or large frying pan.
Fry 4 of the spring onions, the garlic and ginger
for 2 minutes. Push to the side of the pan, add the
carrots and cabbage and fry until softened.

Mix together the chilli sauce, tomato purée, soy
sauce and kecap manis in a small bowl. Add this to
the pan and bubble for a few moments, then stir
through the cooked rice and edamame beans until
warmed through. Add half the coriander.

Heat the remaining oil in a small frying pan and fry
2 or 3 eggs. Divide the rice between shallow bowls.
Top with the fried eggs, the remaining coriander
and spring onion, the peanuts and drizzle with
chilli sauce.

ONE POT

★

JAMBALAYA

Meaning 'jumbled' or 'mixed up', this hotchpotch of French and Spanish cuisine hails from Louisiana. It starts with the 'holy trinity', a sofrito-like mixture so called in Creole and Cajun cooking, which consists of onion, celery and green pepper.

SERVES 6

TAKES about 1 hour

200g/7oz cured chorizo sausage,
  thickly sliced
6 skinless and boneless chicken
  thighs, cut into chunks
1 large onion, finely chopped
1 stick celery, finely chopped
3 mixed colour (bell) peppers,
  roughly chopped
1 tbsp olive oil
3 garlic cloves, crushed
1 tbsp Cajun spice mix
300g/1½ cups long-grain rice
3 sprigs thyme
400g/14oz can chopped tomatoes
650ml/1⅓ pints hot
  chicken stock
5 spring onions (scallions),
  finely sliced
salt and freshly ground
  black pepper

Heat a large lidded frying pan over a medium–high heat. Add the chorizo and fry until it has released its oil and is browned all over. Remove using a slotted spoon and set aside. Add the chicken to the pan and brown for 10–15 minutes, then transfer to the chorizo plate.

Tip the onion, celery and peppers into the pan with the oil and cook for 5–8 minutes, or until softened. Add the garlic and cajun spice mix and cook for 1–2 minutes more. Stir through the rice, making sure it is well coated, season, then return the meat to the pan and throw in the thyme sprigs. Pour over the tomatoes and stock and bring to a simmer. Cover and cook gently for 20–25 minutes, then turn off the heat and leave to steam for 10 minutes. Scatter over the spring onions before serving.

★

SPIRAL PIES

Adding rice soaks up any liquid from the spinach in these little pies, meaning the pastry stays crisp. They're reminiscent of the börek pastries found all over Europe.

🍴 MAKES 4 pies

⏰ TAKES about 1 hour, plus soaking

100g/generous ½ cup short-grain or risotto rice
500g/1lb 2oz spinach
1 tbsp olive oil
1 onion, finely chopped
2 garlic cloves, finely chopped
1 tbsp dried mint
¼ whole nutmeg, freshly grated
125g/4½oz feta, roughly crumbled
8 sheets filo pastry
75g/2½oz melted butter
1 egg, beaten
1 heaped tsp sesame seeds
salt and freshly ground black pepper

Soak the rice in cold water for at least 30 minutes. Heat a large saucepan over a medium heat and tip in the spinach, cover and cook until wilted, stirring once or twice. Transfer to a colander and leave to cool.

Meanwhile, return the pan to a medium–high heat. Add the oil and fry the onion for 5 minutes, then stir through the garlic and drained rice and toast for 2 minutes. Tip into a large bowl and leave to cool. Squeeze the spinach to remove as much liquid as you can, then roughly chop it and add to the rice. Stir through the mint, nutmeg and some seasoning, then gently toss through the feta.

Preheat the oven to 200°C/400°F/gas 6 and line a tray with parchment paper. Lay a filo sheet on your work surface with the longest edge facing you and brush with melted butter. Top with another filo sheet and some more butter. Distribute one-quarter of the spinach mix along the nearest edge of the pastry, then roll up, tucking in the edges, to create a long log shape. Carefully coil into a round and place on the prepared tray. Repeat with the remaining pastry and filling. Brush the spirals with any remaining butter, then glaze with beaten egg. Sprinkle over the sesame seeds and bake for 30 minutes. Leave to cool before serving.

LAMB

★

BIRYANI

This may be time-consuming, but it's well worth the effort. With its layers of fragrant rice, golden onions and succulent spiced lamb, you'll make it again and again.

SERVES 4–6

TAKES about 2 hours, plus marinating

750g/1lb 10oz lamb shoulder, cut into chunks
200g/7oz Greek-style yoghurt
100g/3½oz tikka masala curry paste
75g/2½oz ghee
2 large onions, finely sliced
50g/2oz ginger, peeled and grated
50g/2oz garlic cloves, crushed
6 cardamom pods, seeds crushed
1 tsp ground cinnamon
4 cloves
3 bay leaves
350g/1¾ cups basmati rice
½ tsp saffron, soaked in 100ml/3½fl oz boiling water
2 tbsp chopped coriander (cilantro), plus extra to serve
2 tbsp chopped mint, plus extra to serve
salt and freshly ground black pepper
3 tbsp flaked almonds, toasted (optional)

In a bowl, combine the lamb, yoghurt, curry paste and some seasoning, then cover. Chill for 2 hours.

Heat 50g/2oz of the ghee over a medium–high heat in a large casserole dish. Add the onions and a pinch of salt and fry for 10 minutes until crisp and brown. Remove using a slotted spoon and set aside.

Whiz the ginger, garlic and 2 tbsp cold water to a paste. Add the oil to the casserole dish and fry for 1 minute, then add the spices and bay leaves. Add the meat and marinade, reduce the heat to low and cook for 20 minutes. Pour over 250ml/9fl oz boiling water, cover and simmer for 30 minutes until the meat is tender. Remove the lid and cook for a further 15 minutes until the sauce has thickened.

Meanwhile, bring a large pan of salted water to the boil, add the rice and cook for 8 minutes, then drain.

Preheat the oven to 150°C/300°F/gas 2. Heat the remaining ghee in a large lidded pan, sprinkle over some of the rice and spread out. Top with half the lamb, half the remaining rice, half the saffron, water, half the onions, all the chopped herbs and some salt. Top with the remaining lamb, rice, saffron and onions. Cover with parchment paper and the lid, and bake in the oven for 35–40 minutes until the rice is cooked. Scatter with the herbs and almonds.

GRUYÈRE

★

COURGETTE GRATIN

The red onion, parsley and caper salad cuts through the richness of this Mediterranean dish. It's great for using up a glut of courgettes. Add bacon or chorizo to make it meaty.

SERVES 4

TAKES 55 minutes

200g/1 cup easy-cook
   wholegrain rice
25g/1oz butter, plus extra
   for greasing
1 red onion, finely sliced
850g/1lb 14oz courgettes
   (zucchini), coarsely grated
2 garlic cloves, crushed
250g/9oz mascarpone
100ml/3½fl oz milk
1 heaped tbsp Dijon mustard
100g/3½oz Gruyère, finely grated
salt and freshly ground
   black pepper
For the red onion and caper salad
½ red onion, finely chopped
1½ tbsp capers, roughly chopped
small bunch flat-leaf parsley,
   finely chopped

Bring a large pan of salted water to the boil, tip in the rice and simmer for 15–20 minutes until almost fully cooked, then drain.

Meanwhile, heat the butter in a large frying pan and cook the onion for 8 minutes. Turn up the heat to the highest setting, add the courgettes and cook for 10 minutes. Stir in the garlic and some seasoning, then combine with the rice and set aside to cool.

Preheat the oven to 200°C/400°F/gas 6. In a bowl, mix together the mascarpone, milk, mustard, 75g/2½oz of the Gruyère and some seasoning. Add to the rice and mix well. Transfer to a lightly buttered baking dish and top with the remaining cheese. Bake for 30 minutes until golden and bubbling.

Meanwhile, mix together the ingredients for the salad. Serve alongside the gratin.

ALBANIAN BAKED
★
LAMB & RICE

Tender lamb and rice with oregano, baked under a veil of garlicky yoghurt – this is the national dish of Albania and, although it may sound unusual, it is truly delicious.

🍴 SERVES 4

⏰ TAKES about 2 hours

700g/1lb 9oz boneless lamb shoulder cut into 4–5cm/ 2in pieces
1 tbsp olive oil, plus a little extra
2 tsp dried oregano, plus a little extra
75g/⅓ cup long-grain rice
handful mint leaves
salt and freshly ground black pepper
lettuce and tomato salad, to serve
For the topping
25g/1oz butter
3 garlic cloves, crushed
25g/3 tbsp plain (all-purpose) flour
350g/12½oz Greek yoghurt
3 eggs, beaten
freshly grated nutmeg

Preheat the oven to 180°C/355°F/gas 4. Season the lamb. Heat the oil in a large frying pan over a high heat and brown the lamb really well in batches for 6–8 minutes. Tip the contents of the frying pan into a snug baking dish, pour over 300ml/10½fl oz boiling water, cover tightly with foil and braise in the oven for 1 hour, or until tender. Remove the foil and pour the lamb cooking liquid into a measuring jug – you should have about 330ml/11fl oz (top up with water if needed).

Once the lamb is cooked, make the topping. Melt the butter in a saucepan, then add the garlic and stir for a few moments. Stir in the flour and cook for 1 minute. Slowly whisk in 180ml/6fl oz of the lamb cooking liquid and bubble for 2 minutes. Remove from the heat and whisk in the yoghurt, eggs, nutmeg and some seasoning. Return to the heat and warm through.

Stir the oregano and rice into the lamb and pour over the remaining cooking liquid. Spoon the sauce over the top and sprinkle with extra oregano. Drizzle with a little oil, grind over some black pepper and bake for 30–40 minutes until golden and set. Leave to cool for 5 minutes, then scatter over the mint. Serve with a lettuce and tomato salad.

BLACK RICE WITH

★
SQUID & ALIOLI SAUCE

The rice here isn't black but becomes so with the addition
of squid ink. You'll end up with black lips and teeth after
eating, so it's not ideal for a first date.

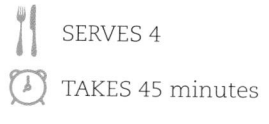

SERVES 4

TAKES 45 minutes

2 tbsp olive oil
350g/12½oz prepared and cleaned
  baby squid, cut into 5mm/
  ¼in rings
2 banana shallots, finely chopped
2 garlic cloves, finely chopped
1 small green (bell) pepper,
  finely chopped
125g/4½oz tomatoes, deseeded
  and finely chopped
1 tsp hot smoked paprika
300g/generous 1½ cups bomba or
  paella rice
1.2 litres/2½ pints hot fish stock,
  plus extra if needed
10–12 sachets (40–50ml/
  1¼–1¾fl oz) squid ink
1 small bunch parsley,
  finely chopped
salt and black pepper
lemon wedges, to serve
For the alioli sauce
4 garlic cloves
150ml/5fl oz extra virgin olive oil
¼ tsp salt

Heat 1 tbsp of the oil in a large frying pan over a
high heat and fry the squid for 1 minute, then tip
it into a bowl and set aside. Add the remaining oil
to the pan and fry the shallots for 5–8 minutes.
Stir through the garlic, green pepper and tomatoes
and cook for a further 5 minutes. Add the paprika
and rice and stir to coat. Pour over the stock, then
squeeze in the squid ink and return the squid to the
pan. Bring to a simmer and cook for 20–25 minutes,
stirring every so often, until the stock has been
absorbed and the rice is al dente. Add more stock
if needed.

To make the alioli, pound the garlic and salt to a
paste in a pestle and mortar. Very slowly trickle
in the oil, continuing to crush the paste with the
pestle as you go. Keep adding the oil and mixing
until you have an emulsified sauce. Add a splash
of milk if it becomes thick.

Season the rice and stir through most of the
parsley. Transfer to plates, spoon over a little of
the alioli and scatter with the remaining parsley.
Sprinkle over a pinch of paprika and serve with
lemon wedges.

MOROCCAN

★

BAKED CHICKEN

A one-pot dish flavoured with spicy rose harissa paste,
olives and dried apricots. Chuck it in the oven and get on
with other business whilst it does its thing.

 SERVES 4

TAKES 1 hour 25 minutes,
plus marinating

2 tbsp olive oil
2 heaped tbsp rose harissa
1½ tsp ground cinnamon
8 chicken thighs, skin on
   and bone in
1 large red onion, sliced
6 garlic cloves, crushed
75g/2½oz flaked almonds
100g/3½oz dried apricots,
   roughly chopped
100g/3½oz pitted green olives,
   roughly chopped
250g/1¼ cups wholegrain
   basmati rice
400g/14oz can chopped tomatoes
550ml/19fl oz hot chicken stock
2 tbsp pomegranate seeds
¼ cucumber, halved, deseeded
   and sliced
handful coriander (cilantro) leaves
salt and freshly ground
   black pepper
Greek yoghurt, to serve

In a large bowl mix together 1 tbsp of the oil,
1 heaped tbsp of the harissa, 1 tsp of the ground
cinnamon and a little salt. Add the chicken and toss
to coat. Chill for at least 2 hours or overnight.

Preheat the oven to 180°C/355°F/gas 4. Heat an
ovenproof sauté pan or casserole dish over a
medium–high heat. Add the remaining oil and fry
the chicken in batches, starting skin-side down,
until golden. Remove using a slotted spoon. Add
the onion to the pan and fry for about 5 minutes
until softened. Stir through the garlic and almonds
and cook until golden, then add the apricots, olives
and remaining ½ tsp ground cinnamon. Spoon in
the remaining harissa and tip in the rice, then pour
over the tomatoes and stock, stir and season. Add
the chicken and its resting juices to the pan, then
bring to a simmer. Cover tightly and cook in the
oven for 1 hour, or until the rice is tender. Check
after 45 minutes and add a little more water
if needed.

Scatter over the pomegranate seeds, cucumber
and coriander. Serve with a bowl of cooling
Greek yoghurt.

CHICKPEA & RICE

★

STUFFED SQUASH

You'll make slightly more of the rice filling than you need –
perfect for lunch the following day with some chicken
and salad leaves.

SERVES 2

TAKES 45 minutes

100g/½ cup plus 1 tbsp mixed
   basmati and wild rice
1 onion squash or small
   butternut squash (550–600g/
   1lb 3oz–1lb 5oz)
1 tbsp olive oil
100g/3½oz canned chickpeas
   (drained weight)
1 small red onion, finely chopped
25g/1oz pomegranate seeds
25g/1oz hazelnuts, toasted and
   roughly chopped
½ tsp cumin seeds, toasted and
   lightly crushed
zest and juice ½ orange
½ small bunch dill, roughly
   chopped
½ small bunch parsley,
   roughly chopped
1 small garlic clove, crushed
3 tbsp tahini
50g/2oz feta
salt and freshly ground
   black pepper

Cook the rice in salted water according to the
packet instructions. Drain, then spread it out on
a tray and leave to cool.

Meanwhile, preheat the oven to 200°C/400°F/gas 6.
Halve the onion squash and scrape out the seeds.
Rub all over, even the skin, with the oil. Season
and roast, cut-side up, for 30–40 minutes, or
until tender.

Combine the rice, chickpeas, onion, pomegranate
seeds, hazelnuts, cumin seeds, orange zest, herbs
and seasoning in a bowl. In a separate bowl, mix
together the garlic, tahini and orange juice with
some seasoning and enough cold water to make a
drizzly dressing – about 1–2 tbsp. Pile the rice into
the roasted squash halves, crumble over the feta
and drizzle with the tahini dressing.

ALOO GOBI
★
TAHARI

A one-pot fragrant rice pilaf. If you're adding rosewater,
make sure it's the delicate Middle-Eastern stuff and not
the highly concentrated variety used for baking.

SERVES 2

TAKES 50 minutes

1½ tbsp ghee or oil
1 large red onion, sliced
1 tsp black mustard seeds
1 tsp cumin seeds
200g/7oz potatoes, cut into
   2.5–3cm/1in chunks
150g/5½oz cauliflower florets
2 garlic cloves, crushed
1 tsp freshly grated ginger
2 tomatoes, roughly chopped
2 tsp curry powder
100g/½ cup plus 1 tbsp
   basmati rice
50g/2oz frozen peas, defrosted
¾ tsp rosewater (Lebanese-style)
   (optional)
300ml/10½fl oz boiling water
25g/1oz cashew nuts, roughly
   crushed
salt and freshly ground
   black pepper
raita or tzatziki, to serve

Heat 1 tbsp of the ghee in a large frying pan over
a medium–high heat. Add the onion and a pinch
of salt and cook for 10 minutes until golden brown.
Add the mustard and cumin seeds and fry until
popping. Remove using a slotted spoon and
set aside.

Add the remaining ghee to the pan and fry the
potatoes and cauliflower for 5 minutes, or until
starting to brown. Stir through the garlic and ginger,
then the tomatoes and cook for 1 minute. Add the
curry powder, rice and some seasoning and stir
to coat. Add the peas, half the cooked onion, the
rosewater (if using) and the boiling water. Cover and
simmer over the lowest heat for 15 minutes, or until
the rice and potatoes are cooked and the water
has been absorbed. Turn off the heat and leave to
steam for 10 minutes

Meanwhile, toast the crushed cashews in a small
frying pan. Fluff the rice before serving topped
with the reserved onion, crumbled cashews and
some raita.

MALTESE

★

BAKED RICE

A traditional dish of Malta, every family has its own secret recipe, which is passed down through the generations.

🍴 SERVES 6–8

⏰ TAKES about 1 hour, plus resting

1 tbsp olive oil, plus extra
   for greasing
200g/7oz smoked bacon lardons
1 onion, finely chopped
1 garlic clove, crushed
1 bay leaf
500g/1lb 2oz beef mince
1 heaped tsp curry powder
350g/1¾ cups long-grain rice
3 tbsp tomato purée
680g/1lb 8oz passata
700ml/generous 1½ pints hot
   beef stock
200g/7oz mature Cheddar
   or Parmesan
3 eggs, beaten
salt and freshly ground
   black pepper
green salad, to serve

Preheat the oven to 200°C/400°F/gas 6. Oil a large baking dish.

Heat the oil in a large frying pan over a medium–high heat. Fry the lardons for 5 minutes until beginning to brown. Add the onion and cook for about 5 minutes until softened, then stir through the garlic and bay leaf. Turn up the heat and tip in the beef mince, breaking it up with a wooden spoon. Cook the mince for about 8 minutes until browned and any liquid has evaporated. Reduce the heat and stir through the curry powder and rice. Add the tomato purée and pour over the passata and stock. Stir and season, then bring to a simmer and cook for 10 minutes.

Stir through 100g/3½oz of the cheese, the beaten eggs and some seasoning. Tip into the prepared baking dish and bake for 20 minutes. Stir, top with the remaining cheese and bake for a further 10–12 minutes, until golden and bubbling. Leave to rest for 15 minutes before serving with a green salad.

SMOKY

★

SPANISH RICE

This dish can be thrown together with whatever vegetables you have to hand. Try using aubergine (eggplant), courgette (zucchini) or butternut squash. Make sure you use a sweet smoked paprika, otherwise it may be too bitter.

SERVES 3–4

TAKES about 1 hour

1 large bulb fennel, cut into
    2.5cm/1in chunks
2 romano peppers, thickly sliced
400g/14oz can artichokes, drained
    and halved
3 large garlic cloves, thickly sliced
1 tsp fennel seeds, lightly crushed
2 tsp sweet smoked paprika
3–4 tbsp olive oil
25g/1oz butter
1 large red onion, thinly sliced
200g/1 cup plus 1 tbsp bomba
    or paella rice
peeled zest ½ lemon, plus lemon
    wedges to serve
400ml/14fl oz hot vegetable stock
3 tbsp capers, drained
1 small bunch parsley,
    roughly chopped
salt and freshly ground
    black pepper

Preheat the oven to 200°C/400°F/gas 6. Tip the fennel, peppers, artichokes, garlic, fennel seeds, paprika and seasoning into a large tray lined with baking parchment. Drizzle over 2 tbsp of the oil, toss together and spread out in a single layer. Roast for 20 minutes.

Meanwhile, heat the butter and the remaining oil in a large lidded frying pan. Add the onion and cook for 5 minutes until softened. Tip in the rice, lemon zest and seasoning and stir for 2 minutes. Pour over the stock, bring to the boil, then turn the heat down. Cover and simmer gently for 20 minutes, or until al dente.

After the vegetables have been roasting for 20 minutes, stir through the capers and roast for a further 20 minutes.

Once the rice is al dente, increase the heat and cook for a further 5 minutes to crisp the base. Remove from the heat and set aside for 5 minutes. Top the rice with the roasted vegetables, sprinkle over the parsley and serve with lemon wedges.

BEEF & RICOTTA
★
STUFFED CABBAGE LEAVES

A popular dish all over the world, with different countries and peoples having their own twists. Adding ricotta to the mince mixture softens the filling of these tasty parcels.

SERVES 4

TAKES 1 hour 20 minutes

85g/½ cup wholegrain
   basmati rice
12–15 savoy cabbage leaves
250g/9oz beef mince
250g/9oz pork mince
1 onion, finely chopped
1 garlic clove, crushed
150g/5½oz ricotta
1 egg, beaten
1½ tsp allspice
1 tbsp dried oregano
½ small bunch mint leaves, finely
   chopped, plus extra to serve
zest 1 lemon
salt and freshly ground
   black pepper
For the sauce
1 tbsp olive oil, plus extra
   for drizzling
1 onion, finely chopped
500g/1lb 2oz passata
2 tsp agave or honey
2 garlic cloves, crushed

Cook the rice in salted water according to the packet instructions. Drain, then spread it out on a tray and leave to cool. Meanwhile, bring a large pan of water to the boil and blanch the cabbage leaves for 3–4 minutes until softened, then drain and leave to cool.

To make the sauce, heat the oil in a saucepan, add the onion and soften for 8 minutes. Tip in the passata and agave and season well. Simmer gently for 10 minutes, partially covered to stop any splattering. Stir through the garlic, then spoon two-thirds of the sauce into a large baking dish.

Preheat the oven to 180°C/355°F/gas 4. Combine the beef and pork mince, onion, garlic, ricotta, egg, allspice, herbs and lemon zest in a bowl. Season and stir in the rice. Lay a cabbage leaf on your work surface and place several generous spoonfuls of the mixture in the centre of it. Roll up the leaf, tucking in the sides. Place on top of the sauce in the dish. Repeat with the remaining leaves and filling. Pour the remaining sauce over the cabbage rolls and drizzle with a little oil. Cover with foil and bake for 30 minutes, then uncover and bake for 10 minutes more. Scatter with mint before serving.

UPSIDE-DOWN
★
RICE CAKE

Maghluba means 'upside down' in Arabic, and this rice cake
is a traditional Palestinian dish that usually includes meat.

🍴 SERVES 6

⏰ TAKES about 2 hours

500g/1lb 2oz Charlotte potatoes,
    sliced just under 1cm/½in thick
5 tbsp olive oil, plus extra for
    greasing
2 tsp ground cumin
2 aubergines (eggplants), sliced
    into 1cm/½in rounds
400g/14oz spinach, blanched in
    boiling water then squeezed out
zest 1 lemon, plus wedges to serve
3 large or 6 smaller tomatoes,
    sliced 5mm/¼in thick
6 garlic cloves, crushed
300g/generous 1½ cups white
    short-grain rice, soaked in cold
    water for 30 minutes
625ml/1⅓ pints hot
    vegetable stock
1 tsp ground turmeric
1 tsp ground cinnamon
1 tsp ground allspice
1 tsp freshly grated nutmeg
handful mint leaves
salt and black pepper
tzatziki, to serve

Preheat the oven to 200°C/400°F/gas 6. Line
two large trays with baking parchment. Toss the
potatoes in a large bowl with 2 tbsp oil, 1 tsp cumin
and some seasoning, then spread out on one of the
trays. In the same bowl, toss the aubergines with
3 tbsp oil and some seasoning, then arrange on the
other tray. Roast the vegetables for 35–40 minutes,
or until golden brown and tender. In a bowl mix the
spinach with seasoning and the lemon zest.

Line the base of a deep 23cm/9in lidded pan with
baking parchment. Grease the pan with oil. Lay the
tomato slices over the base of the pan, then top
with the roasted aubergines. Scatter over one-third
of the garlic, followed by one-third of the drained
rice. Top with the potatoes, then another one-third
of garlic and one-third of rice. Arrange the spinach
on top of the rice and scatter with the final one-
third of garlic and the remaining rice.

Mix together the stock and spices, including the
remaining 1 tsp cumin and 1 tsp salt. Pour this over
the rice and bring to a simmer, then lay a circle of
parchment on top and weigh down with a saucer.
Add the lid, reduce the heat to low and cook for
35 minutes. Turn off the heat and leave to steam
for 20 minutes, then invert onto a plate. Scatter
over the mint leaves and serve with tzatziki.

SPANISH

★

SEAFOOD RICE

A take on the classic Valencian seafood paella. You want the rice to crisp a little on the bottom of the pan – this is called 'socarrat' and is considered a delicacy.

SERVES 4

TAKES about 1 hour

850ml/1¾ pints hot chicken stock
¼ tsp saffron
1 tbsp olive oil
200g/7oz chorizo, sliced
6 rashers smoked streaky bacon, roughly chopped
1 large onion, sliced
3 garlic cloves, crushed
3 plum tomatoes, finely chopped
1 tsp sweet smoked paprika
350g/1¾ cups bomba or paella rice
300g/10½oz mussels, cleaned
300g/10½oz clams, cleaned
250g/9oz raw shell-on prawns (shrimp), cleaned
small bunch parsley, roughly chopped
salt and freshly ground black pepper
2 lemons, cut into wedges, to serve

Pour the stock over the saffron and set aside. Heat the oil in a large paella or frying pan over a medium heat. Add the chorizo and bacon and cook until beginning to crisp. Add the onion and garlic, then lower the heat and cook for 8 minutes until softened. Turn up the heat a little and stir through the tomatoes and paprika, then cook for 5 minutes more. Tip in the rice, season and stir for 2–3 minutes until the rice is golden. Pour over 750ml/1¼ pints of the saffron stock, bring to the boil, cover, then lower the heat and simmer for 15 minutes.

Wash the shellfish and discard any mussels or clams that don't close when tapped. Once the rice is cooked, quickly tip the seafood into the pan and pour over the remaining stock. Cover with the lid again, increase the heat to medium and cook for 10–15 minutes until the mussels and clams have opened and the prawns are pink. Set aside to steam for 10 minutes. Discard any clams or mussels that haven't opened. Scatter over the parsley and serve with lemon wedges.

HONG KONG
★
CLAY POT RICE

This one-pot rice dish is all about the crispy bottom. If you
don't have a clay pot (an unglazed earthenware pot),
a casserole dish or heavy-based pan will work fine.

SERVES 4

TAKES 50 minutes,
plus soaking

300g/generous 1½ cups sushi rice
2 tbsp Shaoxing wine
3 tbsp toasted sesame oil
3 tbsp soy sauce
1 tsp caster (granulated) sugar
1 tbsp cornflour (cornstarch)
thumb ginger, peeled, ½ grated
   and ½ cut into matchsticks
500g/1lb 2oz skinless and boneless
   chicken thighs, cut into chunks
25g/1oz dried shiitake mushrooms
¼ tsp salt
1½ tsp Sichuan peppercorns,
   lightly crushed
5 spring onions (scallions), sliced
   on an angle
3 garlic cloves, sliced

Soak the rice in cold water for 30 minutes.
Meanwhile, mix together the Shaoxing, 2 tsp of
the sesame oil, 1 tbsp of the soy sauce, the sugar,
cornflour and grated ginger in a bowl. Add the
chicken and toss to coat. Cover and chill.

Bring 450ml/16fl oz water to the boil in a casserole
pot with a lid. Add the shiitake mushrooms, cover
and simmer for 10 minutes. Remove the mushrooms
using a slotted spoon. Tip the drained rice into the
water with 1 tsp sesame oil and the salt. Bring to
the boil, lower the heat, cover and simmer for
25 minutes, or until the rice is cooked and a crust
has formed on the bottom. Remove from the heat.

Meanwhile, heat 1 tbsp oil in a wok or large frying
pan over a high heat. Stir-fry the chicken and
its marinade for about 10 minutes, scraping the
bottom of the pan from time to time. Add the
mushrooms and Sichuan peppercorns and fry for
3–4 minutes, or until the chicken is cooked. As soon
as the rice is cooked, tip the chicken over the top.
Cover with the lid and steam for 10 minutes.

Wipe out the wok or frying pan and heat 1 tbsp oil.
Stir-fry the ginger until golden, then add the spring
onions and garlic and cook until crisp. Splash in
2 tbsp soy, then spoon on top of the rice.

JOLLOF-STYLE
★
RICE & FISH

Jollof rice is a traditional West African dish of which the region is very protective. Hopefully this version is as good as the real thing.

SERVES 2

TAKES 55 minutes

125g/scant ¾ cup jasmine rice
1½ tbsp sunflower oil
100g/3½oz shallots, sliced
1 red (bell) pepper, deseeded and
    roughly chopped
½ Scotch bonnet, seeds removed
400g/14oz passata
3 tbsp tomato purée
1 tsp grated ginger
1 large garlic clove, crushed
¼–½ tsp caster (granulated) sugar
200ml/7fl oz hot chicken stock
1 tbsp picked thyme leaves, plus
    extra to garnish
25g/1oz salted plantain chips
2 fillets sea bass or sea bream
salt

Soak the rice in cold water for 30 minutes. Meanwhile, heat 1 tbsp of the oil in a saucepan over a medium–high heat, add the shallots and fry for 8 minutes until softened.

Tip the red pepper, Scotch bonnet, passata, tomato purée, ginger, garlic, ¼ tsp sugar and some salt into a food processor. Blend until smooth. Add this to the shallots and bring to a simmer. Partially cover and cook for 15–20 minutes until reduced and thickened.

Add the drained rice to the sauce and stir for 2 minutes. Pour over the stock, add the thyme, then cover and simmer for 15 minutes, stirring every now and then. Turn off the heat and leave to steam for 10 minutes, taste and add more sugar or salt if needed.

Meanwhile, roughly crush the plantain chips. Heat the remaining oil in a non-stick frying pan. Season the fish and fry skin-side down for 2–3 minutes, or until crispy. Flip over and remove the pan from the heat. Leave the fish in the pan for 2 minutes, or until cooked through, then remove. Spoon the rice onto plates and top with the fish, plantain and a few thyme leaves.

RED RICE, BASIL &

★

RICOTTA STUFFED POUSSINS

Roast poussins make a great alternative to chicken and
everyone can tuck into their own bird. They're much
quicker to cook, too. The stuffing here is delicious!

SERVES 2

TAKES about 1 hour
15 minutes

100g/½ cup red rice, plus 1 tbsp
  olive oil
5 slices Parma ham (prosciutto)
1 onion, finely chopped
1 stick celery, finely chopped
2 garlic cloves, crushed
125ml/4fl oz white wine
100g/3½oz ricotta
25g/1oz Parmesan, finely grated
½ small bunch basil, roughly
  chopped, plus extra to serve
2 poussins
salt and freshly ground
  black pepper
Cavolo nero or salad leaves,
  to serve

Cook the rice in boiling salted water according
to the packet instructions. Preheat the oven to
200°C/400°F/gas 6.

Meanwhile, heat 1 tbsp oil in a large frying pan and
cook 3 slices of the Parma ham until crisp, then
remove and set aside. Add the onion and celery
to the pan and fry for 8 minutes, then stir through
the garlic. Pour in 50ml/1¾fl oz of the wine and
cook until mostly evaporated. Tip the cooked rice
into the pan, then chop the crispy Parma ham and
stir this in too. Set aside to cool a little, then stir
through the cheeses, basil and some seasoning.

Stuff the rice mixture into the cavities of the
poussins. Place in a small roasting tray, spooning
any extra stuffing around the edges. Pour over the
remaining wine, drizzle generously with oil, drape
over the remaining Parma ham and season. Roast
for 40–45 minutes, basting and drizzling with
more oil halfway through, or until the poussins are
cooked. Leave to rest for 10 minutes, then scatter
over some basil leaves before serving with cavolo
nero or salad leaves.

Tip: You can make the rice stuffing in advance
and chill it, but bring it back to room temperature
before using.

SIDE

★

DISHES

JEWELLED

★

RICE

Despite being a side, this fragrant layered Persian rice has the wow factor. It's traditionally made for special occasions and celebrations.

🍴 SERVES 4–6

⏰ TAKES 1 hour 20 minutes

1½ tsp ground cinnamon
10 cardamom pods, crushed
2 tsp cumin seeds, toasted
  and crushed
1½ tbsp dried rose petals, plus
  extra to serve
100g/½ cup caster
  (granulated) sugar
2 carrots, shredded
peeled zest 1 orange
75g/2½oz mixed raisins (golden
  and black)
50g/2oz pistachios, toasted, plus
  extra to serve
50g/2oz flaked almonds, toasted
350g/1¾ cups basmati rice, soaked
  in cold water for 30 minutes
3 tbsp sunflower oil
75g/2½oz butter, plus 25g/1oz
  melted butter
2 large pinches saffron, soaked in
  1 tbsp boiling water
3 tbsp dried barberries
  or cranberries
salt and black pepper

In a small bowl, mix together the cinnamon, cardamom pods, cumin seeds and rose petals, then set aside. Tip the sugar and 250ml/9fl oz cold water into a small saucepan. Bring to the boil, reduce the liquid a little until syrupy, then stir in the carrots. Shred the orange zest, add it to the pan and simmer with the carrots for 4 minutes. Drain and mix with the raisins, pistachios and almonds.

Drain the rice and tip it into a separate saucepan. Cover with boiling water and simmer, covered, for 5 minutes, then drain and set aside.

Heat the oil and the 75g/2½oz butter in a large saucepan or casserole dish. Tip in one-third of the rice, then scatter over one-third of the saffron water, rose petals and spices, fruit and nut mixture, and some seasoning. Continue layering until everything is used up. Wrap the pan lid in a tea towel and cover the rice, making sure the towel is not hanging down. Set over a medium–high heat for 4–5 minutes. Then turn the heat down and cook for 15–20 minutes until the rice is cooked. Remove from the heat and set aside for 10 minutes. Spoon onto a serving platter, drizzle with the melted butter and garnish with the barberries, extra rose petals and roughly chopped pistachios.

LEMON
★
RICE

This is a popular South-Indian side dish with a punchy lemon flavour. Make sure you soak the lentils properly and fry them until really golden or they'll be on the crunchy side.

SERVES 4–6

TAKES 40 minutes

75g/2½oz chana dhal
250g/1¼ cups basmati rice
3 tbsp vegetable or sunflower oil
1 tbsp black mustard seeds
50g/2oz cashew nuts
12 fresh curry leaves
2 green chillies, finely chopped
4cm/1⅝ in piece of ginger, peeled
   and finely chopped
1 tsp turmeric
1 tsp asafoetida
zest and juice 1½ lemons
salt

Soak the chana dhal in boiling water for 30 minutes, then drain. Cook the rice in salted water according to the packet instructions.

Heat the oil in a wok or large frying pan over a high heat. Add the mustard seeds and fry until beginning to pop. Add the chana dhal and fry for 4 mins until golden brown. Throw in the cashews, curry leaves, chillies and ginger and fry for 1–2 minutes until golden. Add the turmeric and asafoetida and stir for 30 seconds. Stir through the rice until well coated and hot, then remove from the heat. Mix in the lemon zest and juice, along with 1¼ tsp salt.

WILD RICE &

★

BACON STUFFING

This wild rice stuffing is fit to grace any Thanksgiving table,
but you'll be making it all year round.

SERVES 6

TAKES about 1 hour

185g/1 cup wild rice
800ml/1⅓ pints chicken stock
50g/2oz dried cranberries,
   roughly chopped
10 rashers of smoked
   streaky bacon
1 onion, finely chopped
2 sticks celery, finely chopped
1 garlic clove, crushed
1 apple, roughly chopped
50g/2oz pecans, roughly broken
1 heaped tbsp picked thyme leaves
large knob butter, plus extra
   for greasing
salt and freshly ground
   black pepper

Cook the rice in the chicken stock according to
the packet instructions. Soak the cranberries in
boiling water.

Lay the bacon in a cold frying pan, then set over
a medium–high heat and fry until crispy. Remove
the bacon, leaving the fat in the pan, and roughly
chop. Gently fry the onion and celery in the bacon
fat for 10 minutes. Add the garlic, apple and pecans
and cook for 8 minutes, or until the apples have
softened. Drain the cranberries and add them to
the pan along with the cooked rice. Stir through
the bacon, thyme and seasoning.

Preheat the oven to 180°C/355°F/gas 4. Tip the
stuffing into a lightly buttered baking dish, dot
with butter, cover with foil and bake for 15 minutes.
Remove the foil and bake for a further 10 minutes.

GALLO

★

PINTO

Eaten morning, noon and night all over Costa Rica and Nicaragua, but both countries dispute the origin of this simple dish of rice and beans. The name translates as 'spotted rooster' in Spanish and refers to the speckled appearance of the dish.

SERVES 4

TAKES 25 minutes

175g/1 cup long-grain rice
2 tbsp coconut or vegetable oil
1 onion, finely chopped
1 red (bell) pepper, finely chopped
2 garlic cloves, finely chopped
1 tsp ground cumin
1 tsp ground coriander
400g/14oz can black beans, rinsed and drained
2 tsp Worcestershire sauce
few shakes of Tabasco
small bunch coriander (cilantro) leaves, finely chopped
salt and freshly ground black pepper

Cook the rice in salted water according to the packet instructions.

Heat the oil in a saucepan and fry the onion and red pepper for 10 minutes. Add the garlic and spices and stir, then turn up the heat a little and tip in the beans. Cook for 4–5 minutes, stirring, until they begin to crisp, then stir in the cooked rice. Add 5–6 tbsp cold water to the pan and warm through. Splash in the Worcestershire sauce and Tabasco. Season and stir through the coriander.

MEXICAN
★
GREEN RICE

A colourful side that's a great accompaniment to a
Mexican meal. Increase or decrease the quantity
of chillies, depending on taste.

🍴 SERVES 4

⏰ TAKES 35 minutes

100g/3½oz spinach
1–2 jalapeño chillies, deseeded
3 shallots, halved
1 large garlic clove
small bunch coriander (cilantro)
small bunch flat-leaf parsley
400ml/14fl oz hot vegetable
    or chicken stock
2 tbsp olive oil
250g/1¼ cups easy-cook
    long-grain rice
salt and freshly ground
    black pepper
1 lime, cut into wedges, to serve

Put the spinach, chillies, shallots, garlic and most
of the herbs into a food processor. Blitz to a paste,
taste and add more chilli, if you like. Add 4 tbsp
of the stock to loosen and blitz again.

Heat the oil in a large saucepan over a high
heat. Add the rice and stir to coat, then fry for
2–3 minutes until starting to turn golden. Tip the
paste into the pan, season well and cook, stirring
for 2 minutes. Pour over the remaining stock and
bring to a simmer, then turn the heat down to the
lowest setting, cover and cook for 15 minutes. Turn
off the heat and leave to steam for 10 minutes. Fluff
with a fork and serve with the reserved herbs and
lime wedges to squeeze over.

CARDAMOM BAKED
★
PILAF RICE

A simple fluffy rice accompaniment that's perfect with
Indian curries. Pop the dish in the oven and forget about it
whilst you get on with the rest of the meal.

🍴 SERVES 6

⏰ TAKES about 1 hour,
plus resting

50g/2oz butter, plus extra
for greasing
1 tbsp sunflower oil
2 onions, finely sliced
10 cardamom pods, lightly bashed
2 tsp cumin seeds
2 sticks cinnamon
2 tsp fennel seeds
2 bay leaves
350g/1¾ cups basmati rice
650ml/1⅓ pints boiling water
salt

Preheat the oven to 200°C/400°F/gas 6. Melt the
butter and oil in a large frying pan over a medium
heat. Add the onions and a pinch of salt and cook
for 10–15 minutes until golden brown. Tip in the
spices and bay leaves and sizzle for 1 minute, then
add the rice and ¾ tsp salt and stir to coat well.
Cook for 2 minutes, then tip into a generously
buttered baking dish. Pour over the boiling water,
cover tightly with foil and bake for 35 minutes.
Remove and rest for 10 minutes before serving.

MUJADARA

★

RICE

An earthy Lebanese rice dish that's perfect with simply cooked lamb or chicken. Any leftovers, which are unlikely, are delicious cold the following day.

SERVES 4–5

TAKES 45 minutes, plus steaming

175g/1 cup jasmine or
   basmati rice
6 tbsp sunflower oil
4 onions, thinly sliced
4 garlic cloves, thinly sliced
2–2½ tsp cumin seeds
2 tsp ground coriander
1 tsp ground cinnamon
400g/14oz can brown lentils,
   rinsed and drained
300ml/⅔ pint hot vegetable stock
4–5 tbsp Greek-style yoghurt
handful mint leaves, roughly torn
salt and freshly ground
   black pepper

Soak the rice in plenty of cold water. Meanwhile, heat half the oil in a large frying pan over a high heat. Fry half the onions with a pinch of salt for about 15 minutes, until caramelised and crispy. Remove using a slotted spoon and spread out on kitchen paper. Repeat with the remaining oil and onions.

Add the garlic and spices to the oil in the pan and cook for 30 seconds. Tip in the lentils and drained rice. Stir to coat, then pour over the stock and add one-third of the fried onions. Cover and simmer for 10 minutes, then turn off the heat and steam for 10 minutes. Season, fluff with a fork and transfer to a serving plate. Dollop and drizzle over the yoghurt, then scatter over the remaining onions, mint and a grinding of black pepper.

PINEAPPLE, GINGER &
★
XO FRIED RICE

Serve this Chinese- and Thai-inspired side in pineapple
halves for a bit of fun.

 SERVES 4–6

TAKES 40 minutes,
plus chilling

225g/1¼ cups jasmine rice
1½ tbsp XO sauce
2½ tbsp light soy sauce
1½ tbsp coconut oil
3 garlic cloves, thinly sliced
2 banana shallots, sliced
1–2 red bird's eye chillies,
   thinly sliced
2.5cm/1in ginger, peeled and
   finely chopped
200g/7oz choi sum or pak choi,
   roughly sliced
300g/10½oz fresh pineapple
   chunks
salt and freshly ground
   black pepper

Cook the rice in salted water according to the
packet instructions. Leave to cool and chill until
cold, ideally overnight.

Stir together the XO and soy sauces and set aside.
Heat the oil in a large frying pan or wok over a
medium–high heat. Fry the garlic until crisp, then
remove using a slotted spoon and set aside. Add
the shallots to the oil and fry for 3–4 minutes
until golden. Add the chillies and ginger and stir for
1 minute, then throw in the choi sum and fry for
2 minutes until the stalks are tender. Spoon in the
sauce mixture and let it sizzle, then add the rice
and pineapple. Stir until coated and hot through.
Taste and season if needed, then top with the
crispy garlic before serving.

YANGZHOU

★

EGG-FRIED RICE

A simple Chinese dish best made with rice that has been
cooked and chilled overnight.

SERVES 4–6

TAKES 40 minutes,
plus chilling

300g/1¾ cups jasmine rice
5 tbsp sunflower oil
3 eggs, beaten and seasoned
100g/3½oz shiitake mushrooms,
   finely sliced
150g/5½oz cooked peeled
   prawns (shrimp)
75g/2½oz frozen peas, defrosted
6 spring onions (scallions),
   finely sliced
1 tbsp sesame oil
2 tbsp Shaoxing wine
4 tbsp soy sauce
handful coriander (cilantro)
   leaves, to serve

Cook the rice according to the packet instructions.
Drain, then spread it out on a tray and leave to
cool. Chill in the fridge until ready to cook,
preferably overnight.

When ready to serve, heat 1 tbsp of the sunflower
oil in a wok until very hot. Add the beaten eggs
and scramble for 30 seconds, then tip onto a
plate. Return the wok to the heat, add 3 tbsp
sunflower oil and heat until nearly smoking. Tip in
the mushrooms and cook for 2 minutes. Add the
last 1 tbsp sunflower oil and the chilled rice. Cook,
stirring for 4–5 minutes, until the rice is starting
to crisp a little here and there. Add the prawns,
peas, scrambled eggs and half the spring onions.
Continue to stir for 2 minutes. Pour in the sesame
oil, wine and soy, adding more soy or sesame oil
to taste.

Serve topped with the remaining spring onions
and coriander.

CARIBBEAN

★

RICE & PEAS

A staple of the Caribbean diet, rice and peas is enjoyed all over the world. It goes with everything, but is particularly good with some spicy jerk chicken.

 SERVES 4

TAKES 35 minutes

5 spring onions (scallions),
  finely sliced
1 whole Scotch bonnet chilli or
  dried habanero
2 garlic cloves, peeled and bashed
4 large thyme sprigs, plus extra
  to garnish
½ heaped tsp allspice
250g/1¼ cups easy-cook
  long-grain rice
400ml/14fl oz can coconut milk
250ml/9fl oz hot vegetable stock
½ tsp salt
400g/14oz can kidney beans,
  rinsed and drained

Tip the spring onions, chilli, garlic, thyme, allspice and rice into a large saucepan. Pour over the coconut milk and stir. Add the vegetable stock and salt, then bring to the boil. Turn down the heat to its lowest setting, cover and simmer for 10 minutes.

Quickly lift the lid and add the kidney beans, cover and cook for a further 10 minutes. Turn off the heat and set aside, covered, for 10 minutes. Stir and serve topped with a few sprigs of thyme.

PERSIAN

★

SAFFRON RICE

This dish is a true delight of buttery fluffy grains of rice.
'Tah-dig' refers to the crispy layer of rice on the bottom of
the pan, which becomes the golden crusty topping when
turned out, and is the bit everyone will fight over.

 SERVES 6–8

TAKES about 1 hour,
plus soaking

450g/2¼ cups basmati rice
2 good pinches saffron
100ml/3½fl oz boiling water
2 tbsp sunflower oil
100g/3½oz butter
salt

Soak the rice in cold water for 30 minutes, then
drain. Soak the saffron in the boiling water.

Bring a large saucepan of salted water to the
boil. Add the rice and simmer for 6–8 minutes,
then drain.

Line the base of a large saucepan with a circle of
parchment paper. Heat the oil and half the butter
in the pan. Tip in half the saffron water, then gently
pile in the rice. Pour over the remaining saffron
water, sprinkle with 1 tsp salt and dot over the
remaining butter. Cover the lid of the pan with a
tea towel, tying it over the top so that it doesn't
hang down, and cook over a medium–high heat for
8 minutes. Reduce the heat and cook for a further
30 minutes. Turn off the heat and leave to steam
for 10 minutes. When ready to serve, invert the
rice onto a plate so that the golden crispy bottom
is on top.

COCONUT, LIME &
★
LEMONGRASS RICE

Use fresh lime leaves if you can to make this fragrant Thai side – you can buy them fresh from some supermarkets or frozen in boxes from Chinese or Thai supermarkets. Store in the freezer and use when needed.

SERVES 4

TAKES 30 minutes

225g/1¼ cups jasmine rice
1 stick lemongrass
3 slices fresh ginger
3 fresh lime leaves
½ tsp salt
350ml/12fl oz coconut milk from a carton (not full-fat from a can)
2 tbsp desiccated (dried shredded) coconut

Wash the rice and tip it into a saucepan. Remove the outer leaves from the lemongrass, halve it lengthways and bash it lightly. Add it to the rice along with the ginger, lime leaves and salt. Pour over the coconut milk and bring to a simmer. Turn down the heat, then cover and simmer for 15 minutes. Remove from the heat and leave to steam for 10 minutes.

Lightly toast the desiccated coconut in a small pan. Transfer the rice to a serving dish, then scatter over the toasted coconut.

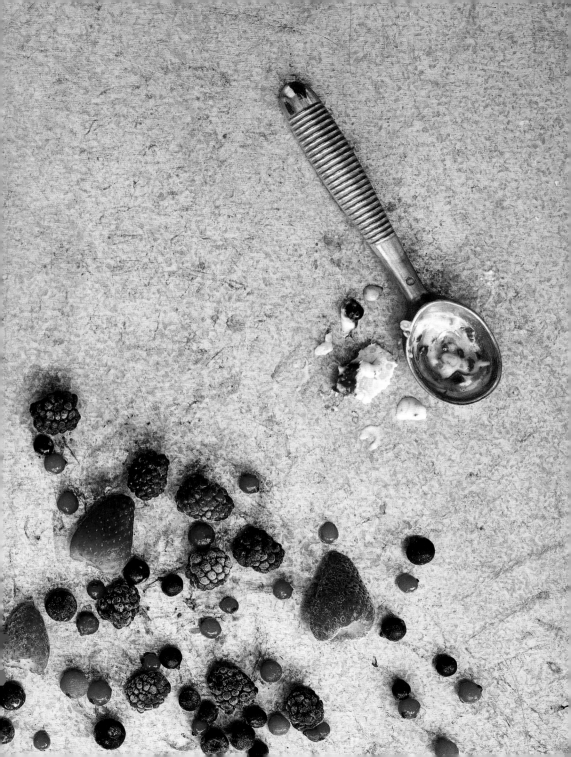

DESSERTS &
★
TREATS

BRÛLÉE-TOPPED

★

BLUEBERRY RICE PUDDINGS

The best bit about this dessert is cracking through the crunchy caramelised sugar topping to reveal what's inside.

SERVES 4

TAKES 45 minutes, plus cooling

200g/7oz blueberries
8½ tbsp caster (granulated) sugar
zest 1 lemon and juice ½ lemon
850ml/1⅓ pints whole milk
½ vanilla pod, halved lengthways and seeds scraped out
pinch of salt
125g/¾ cup pudding rice
2 egg yolks
250g/9oz mascarpone

Tip the blueberries, 3½ tbsp of the sugar and the lemon juice into a small saucepan and stir. Set over a medium–high heat and bring to the boil. Let the berries bubble for 10–12 minutes until they have burst and released their juices and the liquid has reduced. Divide between four 200ml/7fl oz ramekins and leave to cool completely.

Heat the milk, vanilla seeds and pod, and salt in a saucepan. Add the rice and simmer briskly for 20–25 minutes, stirring now and then, until the rice is cooked and creamy. Turn down the heat and remove the vanilla pod.

Beat together the egg yolks, mascarpone, 1 tbsp of the sugar and the lemon zest. Add to the rice and stir continuously for about 4 minutes until thickened. Spoon into the ramekins and leave to cool until just warm and a skin has formed over the top. Sprinkle the top of each pudding with 1 tbsp sugar, then blowtorch or grill until caramelised.

ROASTED PEACHES WITH
★
ARROZ CON LECHE

A Spanish-inspired rice pudding infused with cinnamon and lemon, served chilled with warm honey-roasted peaches and cold cream.

SERVES 2

TAKES 50 minutes, plus chilling

600ml/plus extra 1 pint whole milk, if needed
peeled rind of ½ lemon
1 cinnamon stick
pinch of salt
75g/scant ½ cup bomba or paella rice
1½ tbsp caster (granulated) sugar
½ tsp vanilla bean extract
3 tbsp thick cream
2 peaches
clear honey, for drizzling
large knob butter

Heat the milk, lemon rind, cinnamon and salt in a saucepan. Once simmering, tip in the rice and cook, stirring, for 30–40 minutes, or until the rice is tender. Add more milk if the mixture becomes too thick. Remove from the heat and stir through the sugar, vanilla and 1 tbsp of the cream. Discard the lemon rind and cinnamon stick. Spoon into serving bowls, leave to cool, then chill for 1–2 hours.

When close to serving, preheat the oven to 200°C/400°F/gas 6. Quarter the peaches and place on a parchment-lined baking tray. Drizzle generously with honey and dot with knobs of butter. Roast for 15–20 minutes, basting halfway through, then leave to cool a little.

Top the puddings with the peaches and their syrup, a drizzle of honey and a dollop of cream.

TORTA

DI RISO

Replace the rum with orange juice if you want to
make this Tuscan cake child-friendly. It will keep for
a few days in the fridge.

 SERVES 8–10

TAKES 1 hour 40 minutes,
plus cooling and chilling

butter, for greasing
125g/4½oz sultanas
  (golden raisins)
50ml/1¾fl oz Marsala wine
zest and juice 1 small orange
1 litre/2 pints whole milk
pinch of salt
1 vanilla pod, halved lengthways
  and seeds scraped out
200g/1 cup plus 1 tbsp arborio rice
175g/¾ cup plus 2 tbsp caster
  (granulated) sugar
1½ tsp ground cinnamon
50g/2oz Italian mixed peel
5 eggs, separated
4 heaped tbsp pine nuts
icing sugar, for dusting

Grease and line the base and sides of a deep
20cm/8in round cake tin. Soak the sultanas
in the Marsala and orange juice.

Put the milk, salt and vanilla seeds and pod into a
saucepan, then bring to the boil. Stir in the rice and
simmer briskly for 20–25 minutes, stirring often.
The rice should be cooked, thick and creamy. Leave
to cool.

Preheat the oven to 180°C/355°F/gas 4. Remove
the vanilla pod from the rice and tip the rice into
a bowl. Stir through the sultanas and their soaking
liquid, along with the orange zest, sugar, cinnamon,
mixed peel and egg yolks.

In a separate bowl, whisk the egg whites to medium
peaks. Beat a few tbsp into the rice, then fold
through the rest. Transfer to the prepared tin. Top
with the pine nuts and bake for 1 hour, covering
with baking parchment after 30 minutes. Leave to
cool for 30 minutes in the tin, then remove and
cool completely on a wire rack. Chill, preferably
overnight, before serving. Dust with icing sugar
and slice.

SUMMER BERRY
★
RICE CREAM

There's no churning needed to make this super-creamy frozen dessert. Serve in slices or scoops as the mood takes you.

SERVES 8

TAKES 40 minutes, plus cooling and freezing

700ml/1½ pints whole milk, plus extra if needed
125g/scant ⅔ cup caster (granulated) sugar
pinch of salt
1 vanilla pod, halved lengthways and seeds scraped out
125g/¾ cup pudding rice
500ml/17fl oz double (heavy) cream
150g/5½oz frozen berries
For the compote
350g/12½oz frozen berries
85g/7 tbsp caster (granulated) sugar
juice ½ lemon

Tip the milk, sugar, salt and vanilla seeds and pod into a saucepan. Bring to the boil, add the rice, then turn down the heat and simmer for 25–30 minutes, or until the rice is cooked, stirring every so often. Add a little more milk if needed. Leave to cool.

To make the compote, put all the ingredients into a saucepan and set over a medium heat. Once the sugar has dissolved, simmer vigorously for 10 minutes until jammy, then leave to cool completely.

Brush a 1kg/2lb loaf tin with oil and line it with clingfilm. Remove the vanilla pod from the rice. Whip the cream to soft peaks and beat a few large spoonfuls into the rice, then fold through the rest.

Scatter one-third of the frozen berries over the bottom of the loaf tin and spoon over one-third of the rice, tapping the tin down on the counter to remove any air bubbles. Spoon over half the compote and ripple through. Scatter over one-third of the berries, followed by another one-third of the rice, the remaining compote and berries, finishing with the remaining rice. Cover with clingfilm and freeze for 3–4 hours, or overnight. Take out of the freezer 15 minutes before serving. Turn out and slice with a hot knife, or scoop into balls and serve with the remaining compote.

CARAMELISED BANANAS &
★
BLACK RICE PUDDING

Commonly served for breakfast in parts of Southeast Asia, this also makes a wonderful dessert. Once cooked, the black rice retains some bite and has a nutty taste that goes perfectly with the caramelised banana and cool coconut yoghurt.

🍴 SERVES 2

⏰ TAKES 40 minutes, plus soaking

100g/½ cup Thai black sticky rice (glutinous rice)
400ml/14fl oz coconut milk from a carton (not full-fat from a can)
4½–5 tbsp soft palm or coconut sugar
3 tbsp coconut flakes
2 ripe bananas, thickly sliced
coconut milk yoghurt, to serve
salt

Soak the rice in warm water for at least 30 minutes, then drain. Bring 300ml/10fl oz of the coconut milk to a simmer. Add the rice and a pinch of salt, cover and simmer for 25–30 minutes, or until the rice is cooked. Stir through 1½–2 tbsp of the sugar, depending on taste, and the remaining coconut milk. Cover and set aside.

Toast the coconut flakes in a frying pan until golden, then transfer to a bowl. Heat the remaining sugar with a pinch salt in the frying pan over a medium–high heat. Once melted and bubbly, add the banana slices and cook for about 1–2 minutes on each side until caramelised.

Serve the warm pudding in bowls with a dollop of cold coconut yoghurt, the caramelised bananas and coconut flakes.

SWEET

★

RISOTTO FRITTERS

Often made for festivals, these little balls of deep-fried
sweet risotto are a Tuscan delight. Best served hot and
crisp from the fryer, tossed in lots of sugar.

🍴 MAKES about 30 fritters

⏰ TAKES 55 minutes,
plus chilling

800ml/1⅓ pints whole milk,
   plus extra, if needed
100g/generous ½ cup
   carnaroli rice
pinch of salt
sunflower oil, for deep frying
250g/9oz ricotta, drained
2 eggs, separated
zest 1 orange
75g/2½oz clear honey
3 tbsp rum
2 tsp baking powder
100g/¾ cup 00 flour
100g/½ cup caster (granulated)
   sugar

Bring the milk to a simmer in a saucepan. Add the
rice and salt and simmer briskly for 30–35 minutes,
stirring frequently so that the rice doesn't stick to
the bottom of the pan. When ready the rice should
be thick, soft and creamy. Add a little more milk if
needed. Leave to cool completely, then chill for
3 hours or overnight.

Half fill a large saucepan with oil and start heating.
Line a tray with kitchen paper. Beat the ricotta, egg
yolks, orange zest, honey and rum into the rice,
breaking up any clumps. Stir through the baking
powder and flour. In a separate bowl beat the
egg whites until stiff, then fold these through
the mixture.

Once the oil has reached 180°C/355°F/gas 4, drop
in heaped teaspoonfuls of the batter and fry for
3–4 minutes, turning regularly. Remove using a
slotted spoon and drain on the prepared tray.
Repeat with the remaining batter, then toss the
hot fritters in the sugar and serve warm.

MANGO WITH

⭐

COCONUT STICKY RICE

Using coconut sugar gives the rice a buttery caramel flavour.
If you don't have it or would prefer the rice to remain
white, use caster sugar. You may need less, so add 1 tbsp
at a time and taste. There should be a good balance of
sweet and salt.

SERVES 4

TAKES 50 minutes, plus
soaking and cooling

200g/1 cup Thai sticky rice
   (glutinous rice)
400ml/14fl oz can coconut milk
3½ tbsp coconut sugar, plus 2 tsp
160ml/5½fl oz can coconut cream
1 tsp cornflour (cornstarch)
2 ripe mangoes, sliced
1 tbsp black and white sesame
   seeds, toasted
few small mint leaves
salt

Soak the rice in cold water for at least 3 hours
but preferably overnight, then drain. Line a steamer
with a clean thin cloth and tip in the rice. Pop
on the lid and place the steamer over a pan of
simmering water. Steam for 30 minutes. Remove
from the heat and set aside, covered, for
10 minutes.

Transfer the rice to a bowl. Heat the coconut milk
with 3½ tbsp sugar and the salt. Once the sugar has
dissolved, bring to a simmer, then pour this over
the rice. Cover and cool to room temperature.

When ready to serve, heat the coconut cream in a
small pan with 2 tsp sugar and a few pinches of salt.
Mix the cornflour with 1 tbsp cold water and whisk
into the cream. Heat gently until thickened. Spoon
the rice into serving bowls, arrange the mango
alongside, then pour over the sauce and scatter
with the sesame seeds and mint.

PHIRNI

★

POTS

A chilled North-Indian rice pudding made by simmering ground basmati rice in milk. It's traditionally served in clay pots. Try adding fruit pulp, like alphonso mango purée, to the cooled mixture before chilling.

SERVES 4

TAKES 20 minutes, plus soaking and chilling

50g/¼ cup basmati rice
525ml/18fl oz whole milk
2 pinches saffron
50g/¼ cup caster (granulated) sugar
¼ tsp ground cardamom seeds
pinch of salt
1½ tsp rosewater (Lebanese-style)
To garnish
1 tbsp pistachios, thinly sliced
1 tbsp whole almonds, thinly sliced
1 tsp dried rose petals

Soak the rice in cold water for 30 minutes. Heat 2 tbsp of the milk and pour over the saffron, then set aside.

Drain the rice and transfer to a food processor or spice grinder with another 2 tbsp milk. Blitz until finely ground but still with some texture. Tip the remaining milk into a saucepan and bring to a simmer. Turn down the heat, add the ground rice and immediately start whisking. After 3 minutes, whisk in the soaked saffron, sugar, cardamom and salt. Whisk continuously for about 7 minutes whilst the mixture bubbles and thickens and the milk has reduced by half – it should be the consistency of pourable custard.

Remove from the heat, stir through the rosewater and spoon into serving bowls. Leave to cool, then chill for about 2 hours until set. Top with the nuts and rose petals and serve.

SLOW-BAKED

★

TRADITIONAL RICE PUDDING

You could turn up the oven temperature to cook this pudding more quickly, but there's something about the long, slow cooking and the aromas that fill the house that makes the wait worthwhile.

🍴 SERVES 6

⏰ TAKES 3 hours

800ml/1⅔ pints whole milk
300ml/⅔ pint double (heavy)
   cream
1 vanilla pod, halved lengthways
   and seeds scraped out
¼ heaped tsp freshly
   grated nutmeg
3 tbsp caster (granulated) sugar
100g/generous ½ cup pudding rice
25g/1oz butter, plus extra
   for greasing
strawberry jam, to serve

Preheat the oven to 140°C/275°F/gas 1. Tip the milk, cream, vanilla seeds and pod, nutmeg and sugar into a saucepan. Gently bring to a simmer, then add the rice and stir.

Lightly butter a 1.2 litre/2 pint baking dish and tip in the rice mixture, then dot over the butter. Bake for 30 minutes, stir, then bake for a further 30 minutes and stir again. Return to the oven for 1 hour 30 minutes–1 hour 45 minutes until the pudding is soft, creamy and has a golden skin on top. If it seems too loose, return to the oven for 15 minutes. Leave to cool a little before serving warm with spoonfuls of strawberry jam.

CHOCOLATE

★

RICE PUDDING TART

The texture from the rice adds an extra dimension to the filling, which takes this chocolate tart to another level.

SERVES 10–12

TAKES 1 hour 50 minutes, plus chilling

375g/13oz block shortcrust pastry
plain (all-purpose) flour,
    for dusting
500ml/18fl oz whole milk,
    plus extra if needed
pinch of salt
100g/generous ½ cup pudding rice
100g/4oz 70% dark chocolate,
    chopped
150ml/5fl oz double (heavy) cream
1 tsp vanilla extract
85g/7 tbsp caster (granulated)
    sugar
1 egg and 2 egg yolks, beaten
    together
cocoa powder, for dusting

Roll out the pastry on a floured surface and use it to line a 23cm/9in deep tart tin, leaving a 1cm/½in overhang. Prick the base with a fork and chill for 30 minutes until firm.

Tip the milk and salt into a saucepan and bring to a simmer. Tip in the rice and simmer briskly for 20–25 minutes, stirring often, until cooked and creamy. Add a little more milk if needed. Stir through the chocolate, then leave to cool to room temperature.

Preheat the oven to 200°C/400°F/gas 6. Line the pastry case with baking parchment and fill with baking beans. Bake for 20 minutes. Remove the beans and paper and return to the oven for 10–15 minutes, or until the pastry is golden. Use a sharp knife to cut off the overhang.

Mix the cream, vanilla, sugar and eggs into the rice pudding. Return the tart case to the oven. With the door open, pour the rice filling into the pastry case. Bake for 25–30 minutes, or until set – there should be a slight wobble in the centre. Leave to cool, then chill. Dust with cocoa powder before serving.

CRISPY CHOCOLATE

★

& COCONUT BARS

A sophisticated version of a childhood favourite, chocolate rice crispy cakes. With coconut oil, nut butter and brown puffed rice, you'll be justified in feeling virtuous.

MAKES 15 bars

TAKES 20 minutes, plus chilling

150g/5 cups puffed brown rice
2½ tbsp coconut oil
100g/3½oz honey
125g/4½oz almond butter
3 tbsp cocoa powder
pinch of salt
For the topping
2½ tbsp coconut oil
200g/7oz 70% dark chocolate
25g/1oz desiccated (dried shredded) coconut
sea salt

Lightly grease and line a 20cm/8in square tin with baking parchment. Tip the puffed rice into a large bowl. In a small pan, melt together the oil, honey, almond butter, cocoa powder and salt, stirring until smooth. Pour over the rice and stir to coat. Transfer to the prepared tin and push down firmly with the back of a spoon to level. Chill for 30 minutes.

For the topping, melt together the oil and chocolate until smooth, either in the microwave or in a heatproof bowl over a pan of simmering water. Pour over the chilled base, then scatter the desiccated coconut and a little sea salt on top. Chill for 30 minutes or until firm, then cut into bars.

INDEX

★ ★

THANK YOU

To my family and friends for being my chief tasters, and to Tom for never complaining about the mountains of rice he had to consume.

To Alex Luck for his brilliant photography and Alexander Breeze for his wonderful prop styling. To Sarah Lavelle and everyone at Quadrille for making this book happen, especially Gemma Hayden, Harriet Butt, Helen Lewis, Corinne Masciocchi, Tom Moore and Vincent Smith.

Emily